Macmillan/McGraw-Hill

Read-Aloud Anthology

Social Studies • Grade 6

- Biographies and Autobiographies
- Epics
- Folk Tales, Fables, and Legends
- Interviews
- Journals and Diaries
- Letters
- Nonfiction Selections
- Plays
- Speeches
- Stories

Macmillan McGraw-Hill

New York   Farmington

Acknowledgments

Excerpt from SEEING EARTH FROM SPACE by Patricia Lauber. Copyright © 1990 Patricia Lauber. Orchard Books, a division of Franklin Watts, Inc. NY.

"Scenes from the Stone Age" from an article in TIME MAGAZINE 2/13/95, Vol. 145 by Robert Hughes. Copyright © 1995 Time Inc., Time Magazine.

"First Fruits of the Field" from HIDDEN STORIES IN PLANTS. Kabyle legend retold by Anne Pellowski. Copyright © Anne Pellowski. Macmillan Publishing Company, Inc. NY.

"A Letter from a Han Emperor" from GEMS OF CHINESE LITERATURE. Wen Ti, translated by Herbert A. Giles. © 1884 Bernard Quaritch, Kelly & Walsh, London, Shanghai.

Excerpt from "The Birds" from ARISTOPHANES. Translated by Dudley Fitts. Copyright © 1959, 1962 Dudley Fitts. Harcourt, Brace & World, Inc., NY.

"The Eruption of Mount Vesuvius" from PLINY, LETTERS. Printed in VOICES OF THE PAST. An original translation by James H. Hanscom. Copyright © 1967 The Macmillan Company, NY.

"An Islamic Hospital" from A MEDICAL HISTORY OF PERSIA AND THE EASTERN CALIPHATE by Cyril Elgood. Copyright © 1951, reprint 1979 by Cambridge University Press, London, UK.

Excerpt from THE TERRA COTTA ARMY OF EMPEROR QIN by Caroline Lazo. Copyright © 1993 by Caroline Lazo. Published by Macmillan, New York.

Excerpt from AÏDA retold by Leontyne Price. Copyright © 1990 by Leontyne Price. Published by Harcourt Brace, San Diego, CA.

Excerpt from "Howard Carter's Diary" from FAMOUS SCIENTIFIC EXPEDITIONS by Raymond Holden. Copyright © 1955 by Raymond Holden. Published by Random House, New York.

"Tortoise, Hare, and the Sweet Potatoes" from ASHLEY BRYAN'S AFRICAN TALES, UH-HUH. Copyright © 1998 by Atheneum Books for Young Readers, New York.

Excerpt from THE ART OF KEEPING COOL by Janet Taylor Lisle. Copyright © 2000 by Janet Taylor Lisle. Published by Atheneum Books for Young Readers, New York.

Excerpt from GANDHI by Leonard Everett Fisher. Copyright © 1995 by Leonard Everett Fisher. Published by Atheneum Books for Young Readers, New York.

Excerpt from MANSA MUSA by Khephra Burns. Copyright © 2001 by Khephra Burns. Published by Harcourt, Inc., San Diego, CA.

ATLANTIS, THE LEGEND OF A LOST CITY retold by Christina Balit. Copyright © 1999 by Christina Balit. Published by Henry Holt and Company, New York.

(continued on page 135)

Macmillan/McGraw-Hill

A Division of The **McGraw·Hill** Companies

TABLE OF Contents

UNIT

UNIT 2: THE ANCIENT WORLD   29

UNIT

5

UNIT 5: A STORMY CENTURY   **99**

The readings in the *Macmillan/McGraw-Hill Social Studies Anthology* have been carefully selected to enhance social studies concepts and to provide enjoyable and worthwhile reading experiences for students. All readers bring to the reading experience their own backgrounds and prior knowledge. Exposing students to a variety of viewpoints while encouraging them to question and ponder what they read will help them to become critical readers and thoughtful citizens.

The readings include **primary sources, secondary sources** and **literature.** These fall into several categories, including:

- songs
- official documents
- oral histories
- posters
- diaries and journals
- photographs and graphics
- personal recollections
- political cartoons

- poems
- folktales
- letters
- autobiographies and biographies
- newspaper articles
- fiction and nonfiction
- speeches

The readings offer you a unique teaching tool. The following suggestions will help your students use the readings to build and extend their knowledge of social studies as well as to sharpen their analytical skills.

PRIMARY AND SECONDARY SOURCES

A **primary source** is something that comes from the time that is being studied. Primary sources include such things as official documents of the time, diaries and journals, letters, newspaper articles and advertisements, photographs, and oral histories. A **secondary source** is an account of the past written by someone who was not an eyewitness to those events. Remind students of the difference between primary and secondary sources. Point out that primary sources give historians valuable clues from the past because they provide firsthand information about a certain time or event. Primary sources let the reader see how people lived, felt, and thought.

However, primary sources express the view of only one person. Thus, it is important for students to understand the point of view of the writer and to find out all that they can about his or her background to decide whether the writer is credible, or believable. Secondary sources often compare and analyze different points of view and give a broader view of the event. Once again, however, it is important for students to understand the writer's point of view and analyze his or her credentials. Suggest to students that, when they read primary and secondary sources, they ask themselves these questions:

- Who created the source?
- Can the writer be believed?
- Does the writer have expert knowledge of the subject?
- Does the writer have a reason to describe the events in a certain way?
- Does the writer have a reputation for being accurate?

When you work with the primary sources in this Anthology, you may wish to encourage students to think about the following as they read some of the various sources:

Diaries and Journals Was the diary or journal originally written to be shared with the public? Was it commissioned by a government official, such as the Columbus log was?

Speeches Was the intent of the speech to persuade the audience to adopt a particular point of view or was the speech merely informative? Was the speech delivered during a critical time in a nation's history? Did historical circumstances influence the speechmaker?

Newspaper Articles Did the newspaper in which the article appeared have a particular political stance or bias that might have influenced the writer?

Official Documents Are there any words or phrases in the document that you do not understand? If so, what other source can you consult for clarification?

LITERATURE

In social studies, literature is used to motivate and instruct. It also plays a large role in assisting students to understand their cultural heritage and the cultural heritage of others. For example, the folktales included in the *Macmillan/McGraw-Hill Social Studies Anthology*, such as "Tortoise, Hare, and the Sweet Potatoes" from Africa, were chosen to offer students glimpses of the wisdom various cultures deem important to impart. The songs, stories, and poetry of different cultures offer students opportunities to compare and contrast and hence understand aspects of cultural identity. Epics, such as *The Illiad*, give students opportunities to view ancient history from a classic perspective that has endured through the ages and offers teaching opportunities to integrate history with writing, drama, and art projects.

This year you will be reading about many different peoples, places, and times in your Social Studies textbook. This Anthology, or collection of documents created by different people, will make the information in your textbook come to life in a special way. It includes diaries, songs, stories, plays, posters, poems, speeches, and even ancient pictographs and hiero-glyphics. As you read and study these primary sources, you will be able to see and hear what it was like to live in other times and places. The documents in this Anthology will help you to better understand the world around you and the people—famous and nonfamous—who have shaped our world.

INTRODUCTION •
Gives you background information about the selection and tells you what kind of document it is. Is it fiction or nonfiction? Is it a poem or a song? The introduction also asks you a question to think about as you read the document.

TEXTBOOK LINK •
Tells you which chapter and lesson in your textbook the document is linked to

DEFINITIONS •
Gives you the meanings of difficult words

CONCLUSION •
Provides additional information and asks you to think further about the selection

SOURCE •
Tells you where the selection came from

Use with Chapter 9, Lesson 3

An Islamic Hospital

by Abdul-Wáhid al-Marrakhshi, about 1200

Between the late 700s and the 1200s, Islamic culture became very powerful and influential. The Muslim caliphate, centered in Baghdad, ruled many lands in parts of western Asia, northern Africa, and southern Europe. The people of the Islamic civilization were known for outstanding achievements in many areas including medical care. Ibn Sina (IHB un SEE nuh) (980–1037), a Muslim doctor, wrote medical textbooks with ideas that were far ahead of their time. His contributions to medical knowledge are still recognized as valuable. The following selection by Abdul-Wáhid al-Marrakhshi (ab dul WAY ihd al ma rak SHEE) describes one of the most famous Islamic hospitals, at Marrakesh, Morocco, in North Africa. As you read, consider how this hospital might differ from a modern hospital.

Here was constructed a hospital, which I think is unequalled in the world. First there was selected a large open space in the most level part of the town. Orders were given to architects to construct a hospital as well as possible. So the workmen **embellished** it with a beauty of sculpture and ornamentation even beyond what was demanded of them. All sorts of suitable trees and fruit trees were planted there. Water there was **in abundance**, flowing through all the rooms....

A daily allowance of thirty **dinars** was assigned for the daily ration of food, exclusive of the drugs and chemicals which were on hand for the preparation of **draughts, unguents, and collyria.** For the use of the patients there were provided day-dresses and night-dresses, thick for winter, thin for summer.

After he was cured, a poor patient received on leaving the hospital a sum of money **sufficient** to keep him for a time. Rich patients received back their money and clothes. In short, the Founder did not **confine** the use of the hospital to the poor or to the rich. **On the contrary**, every stranger who fell ill at Marrakesh was carried there and treated until he either recovered or died. Every Friday the Prince after the mid-day prayer mounted his horse to go and visit the patients and to learn about each of them. He used to ask how they were and how they were being treated. This was his use until the day of his death.

The Islamic government also had "moving hospitals" that took beds and medical supplies by camel to places where patients could not get to a hospital.

Source: Cyril Elgood, *A Medical History of Persia and the Eastern Caliphate.* London: Cambridge University Press Associated, 1951 Reprint 1979.

47

embellished: decorated

in abundance: plentiful

dinars: gold coins

draughts, unguents, and collyria: medicines

sufficient: enough

confine: restrict
On the contrary: instead

THE WORLD AND ITS PEOPLE

We are all, every person in the world, aboard the same ship. And so we must all, in ways large and small, treasure and protect it.

Patricia Lauber, 1990

Seeing Earth from Space

by Patricia Lauber, 1990

The study of geography tells us that Earth is divided into regions. There are physical regions, climate regions, cultural regions, and political regions. When astronauts see Earth from space, however, the only borders visible are between the land, sea, and sky. As you read this excerpt from Seeing Earth from Space *by Patricia Lauber, think about the astronauts' view of Earth from space. How might this sight change a person's viewpoint about the planet? How could seeing the planet as a single island in space help different cultures work together for the good of all?*

The Apollo astronauts who landed on the moon found themselves in a strange new world. No one had walked this ground before; the only footprints were their own. Nowhere was there a trace of life other than their own, only craters, seas of hardened lava, hills, and rocks. Above them stars and planets shone with a brilliance never seen on Earth, for the moon has no atmosphere to dim their light. Yet for the astronauts the most exciting sight was Earth. It was more than home.

Seen from the surface of the airless, barren moon or from the orbiting spacecraft, Earth was an island of life in the black sea of space, the only outpost of life to be seen. All the men and women who have flown in space—Americans, Soviets, foreign guests—have been awed by the beauty of the earth. They have also been surprised by its size. To a person standing on its surface, the earth appears both large and sturdy. From space it seems small and fragile.

These men and women are often concerned by the man-made changes they see on the earth. They look down at the island of Madagascar, where tropical forests are being felled. They see that the ocean around it is red-brown, colored by soil eroding from land without trees and carried to the sea by rivers.

They look down and see the slick of an oil spill in the sea. They think about the birds and fishes and mammals and plants that will die and about beaches with tarry sands. They know that from Earth the atmosphere seems to be boundless, an ocean of air that we take for granted and breathe without thinking about it. From space they see that the atmosphere is only a thin shell surrounding the earth. Just before sunrise and just after sunset they can see it—the red layer is the air we breathe; above it is the stratosphere; the blue layer is the ionosphere. Beyond the shell is space, black and empty.

Space travelers often return with their thinking changed. On Earth we think of boundaries. The view from space is different. Rivers meander or rush from country to country without stopping, on their way to the sea. Forests reach from one country into another. Sand and dust from the Sahara spread across the Atlantic and blow toward the Americas. Smoke travels hundreds of miles on the winds. An ocean stretches from continent to continent, and the same waters wash the shores of both.

Space travelers see that the earth is one planet, small and fragile, wondrous and lovely. It is the spaceship in which we journey around the sun, and our life-support system is its air and waters and lands. We are all, every person in the world, aboard the same ship. And so we must all, in ways large and small, treasure and protect it.

Author Patricia Lauber has written many science books for young people. Included among her more than ninety books are The News About Dinosaurs, Tales Mummies Tell, *and* The Eruption and Healing of Mount St. Helens. *Lauber says, "We share the world as if we are on a spaceship. It has everthing we need—air, food, water. We all breathe the same air and drink the same water. When one person pollutes, it affects everyone. We have to see what we are doing to the planet."*

Source: Patricia Lauber, *Seeing Earth From Space.* Orchard Books, 1990.

Easter Island

by Thor Heyerdahl, 1989

Archaeologists and anthropologists often find themselves trying to solve mysteries. Anthropologists are scientists who study human history. For many years one of the world's greatest mysteries lay on a tiny Polynesian island in the Pacific Ocean. This island is more than 1,500 miles (2,400 km) from any other inhabited place. It is named Easter Island. Thousands of years ago people settled there and developed a unique culture that included a written language and remarkable buildings.

When Europeans first reached Easter Island in 1722, they were amazed by what they saw. They found hundreds of gigantic stone statues standing on cliffs and hillsides overlooking the Pacific Ocean. Some of these statues—which consisted of heads, crowns, and bodies without legs—were as tall as a four-story building! Near these statues lay wooden tablets, carved with writing symbols. Where, the Europeans wondered, did these statues come from? How were these statues—some weighing as much as 50 tons (45,000 kg)—moved into their standing positions?

In 1955 an anthropologist from Norway named Thor Heyerdahl (hī ur DAHL) visited Easter Island to try to find the answers to these mysteries. As you read his account of this trip, notice the skills and cooperation that the Easter Islanders demonstrated in order to carve a moai *(MOH ih)—their word for statue. What does Heyerdahl think of the islanders' explanations of how the* moai *moved?*

The mayor [of Easter Island] was sitting on the floor, chipping away at a [statue of a] bird-man figure, when I entered his modest village home. He was known as by far the best sculptor on the island. . . . He was an amazing character. His brain was as sharp as his face, and he was always prepared to find a solution to any problem.

Did he know how his ancestors carved and raised the big *moai?* Of course. If he knew, was he willing to show me? Yes, how big did I wish the *moai* to be? If it was to be big, he would need help from some of the [other] men. . . .When I asked him why, if he knew, he had not revealed his secret to all those who had asked the same question before me, he answered calmly, "Nobody asked *me.*"

In my subsequent dealings with the Easter Islanders I was to understand that this reply was **symptomatic** of the local character. They don't give away anything precious unless you ask for it directly. And anything hidden and not known to others is a treasure. . . .

One night all the members of the expedition were wakened in their tents by the strangest choral singing any of us had ever heard— beautifully harmonized, but almost eerie and totally unlike any music we knew. It was the mayor and his family, who had come to perform an ancient ceremony essential to the success of their enterprise the following day, when they proposed to demonstrate how the work in the quarry was done. A child danced in a paper bird-man mask. Early next morning the mayor and his closest relatives had collected a large number of the stone pickaxes that had lain strewn about the quarry ever since the day work suddenly stopped. They held the picks in their hands, and when the points wore down they sharpened them again simply by chipping off pieces with another stone axe of the same kind. The name for these tools on Easter Island was *toki*, and *toki* is also the ancient word for stone axe among the aboriginal population of North Chile.

After three days' work, the outline of a statue had begun to take shape. . . . No tools were used except the hard [stone] *toki* and water bottles made of **gourds**. The workers constantly sprayed the surface with water to soften up the rock, the interior of which was very hard. . . .

By the third day, we began to see the complete **contour** of the *moai*. We did not have enough time to see them finish the carving, but calculated that it would take about a year for a medium-sized *moai*. There had to be elbowroom between the sculptors, who stood side by side, which meant that the number of men who could work on each statue at one time was very limited. . . .

When I asked the successful mayor how the statues had been moved the long distance from the quarries, he answered, with natural conviction, "The *moai* walked."

These people had been giving that same answer to the same question ever since the first missionaries had asked it. I did not, of course, take the answer seriously. . . . [Perhaps the *moai* had been dragged, I said.]

"This was not the way it was done," said the islanders.

Leonardo was the name of one of those who argued that the stones had walked in an upright position. It sounded so meaningless that I would long since have forgotten the episode had I not written it down in my own book on the expedition at the time.

"But, Leonardo," I said, "how could they walk when they had only heads and bodies and no legs?"

"They wriggled along like this," said Leonardo, and gave a demonstration by edging himself along the rock with feet together and stiff knees.

Upon learning that the word toki—meaning "stone ax"—had the same meaning among both the people of Easter Island and those in northern Chile, Thor Heyerdahl was provided with an important clue. Perhaps the first settlers on Easter Island had come from South America. This theory gained further support when the statues on Easter Island were found to be similar to ancient carvings done by the inhabitants of Peru. These discoveries provided one answer to the questions surrounding the origins of the people of Easter Island. Some anthropologists reject Heyerdahl's theory. They believe that the island's original inhabitants, instead of being South American, were Polynesian sailors from the west.

By watching carefully, Heyerdahl also learned how the people of Easter Island carved the moai. *But what did the islanders mean when they said that the* moai *had walked? Like the missionaries who had come before him, Heyerdahl dismissed their explanation. Then, in the 1980s, an engineer from Czechoslovakia named Pavel Pavel believed he understood what the islanders meant. In 1986 Heyerdahl returned to Easter Island with Pavel. In the account below, Heyerdahl describes what happened.*

It was a great day with an air of suspense and nervous anticipation among the islanders when all was ready for Pavel Pavel to show us how a *moai* could walk. None of the elders doubted that their ancestors had formerly made the statues perform. . . . Old Leonardo was as sure now as he had been thirty years before: the legless stone busts had walked by wriggling forward from side to side. And again he showed us the motion, with the soles of his feet put together, before we had told him or anybody else about the experiment we were to conduct. . . .

Leonardo's sister Elodia . . . sang in a low voice a **monotonous** song in a jerky tempo that matched Leonardo's movements. While she sang an old text and tune she obviously knew by heart, her brother made a string figure like a cat's cradle, which he swung in time to the song. This was repeated during the actual experiment as a kind of magical **invocation**.

monotonous: repetitive

invocation: prayer

The islanders refused to help Pavel until they had observed the ancient custom of baking a pig and sweet potatoes in an **umu** earth oven. . . .

umu: islanders' name for an oven

Pavel had indeed worked out the **ingenious** technique by which the statues were moved—the same technique that we use ourselves to "walk" a heavy refrigerator or a stone too big to carry unaided. . . . All that was needed were four ropes. Two were attached to the top of the statue and used to pull it to each side alternately, while the other two were fastened down at the base and alternately pulled forward. As one team pulled on the top rope to make the statue tilt to the right, the other team pulled the left-hand side of the base forward before the giant tipped back again. The teams then changed sides, causing the **colossus** to waddle along like a drunken man. The technique required great precision and intensive training, but was incredibly effective when the waddling became rhythmic. We reckoned that a well-drilled team of fifteen men could make a twenty-ton [18,000 kg] statue "walk" at least an average of [one] hundred yards [90 m] a day. . . .

ingenious: clever

colossus: gigantic statue

We all felt a chill down our backs when we saw the sight that must have been so familiar to the early ancestors of the people around us. A stone colossus of an estimated ten tons [9,000 kg] "walking" like a dog on a leash. . . . After the successful performance, we all embraced a beaming Pavel Pavel. And Leonardo and Elodia willingly accepted part of the honor. We could all read from Leonardo's face that he had known the truth the whole time: it was the song he and Elodia had sung that had made the *moai* move.

The statue had indeed walked. I could find no better word for it in any European language. I suddenly had an idea. The Easter Island verb for "walk" is *haere*. But when the *moai* started to move, the old islanders used the verb *neke-neke*. I looked this up in [a] dictionary of the Easter Island language, and read: "*neke-neke*: to inch forward by moving the body, due to disabled legs or the absence thereof."

What other language in the world would have a special word for walking without legs? . . .

The technical problems behind the great stone giants were solved. The mysteries that had [long puzzled] visitors and . . . scientists . . . existed no more. The **genesis** of the blind giants dotting the slopes . . . was known, and how they walked. . . . The way each of these incredible feats had been accomplished with help from neither machinery or outer space—all these former puzzles now had their answers.

genesis: origin

One big question emerged: Why had nobody but the islanders themselves taken their ancestral traditions seriously? They would have given us all these answers. I confessed to my two friends that the value of the local oral history was, in a sense, one of the strangest discoveries we had made. A hundred years ago the Easter Islanders had answered all the questions that were put to the elders among them. We from the outside world had recorded what they told us, and saved the answers as primitive fairy-tales. . . .

Thor Heyerdahl believed that he had solved many mysteries during his stays on Easter Island in 1955 and 1986. He concluded that South Americans had traveled great distances across the Pacific Ocean long before Europeans had begun exploring the seas. Heyerdahl learned how the giant statues were made and how they "walked." But he could not solve every mystery. The carved writings on wooden tablets on Easter Island have not yet been translated.

Perhaps Heyerdahl's major discovery was understanding the importance of the stories and oral traditions handed down by people for hundreds of years. As you have learned, many types of documents can teach us about cultures and civilizations throughout the world. Newspapers, hot off the morning presses, and stone monuments thousands of years old—as well as songs, poems, tales, speeches, oral histories, and other types of documents—all provide clues about the world around you. By learning to understand these many sources of information, you can gain a better understanding of the world and prepare for the challenges of tomorrow.

Source: Thor Heyerdahl, *Easter Island: The Mystery Solved*. New York: Random House, Inc., 1980.

EARLY HISTORY

We were but on the threshold of our discovery. What we saw was merely an antechamber. Behind the guarded door there were to be other chambers, possibly a succession of them, and in one of them, beyond any shadow of a doubt, we would find the Pharoah lying.

Howard Carter, 1922

OLD STONE AGE CAVE PAINTINGS

about 18,000 B.C.

During the Old Stone Age, people began to develop the idea that pictures, or symbols, could stand for objects. Soon Old Stone Age artists began to draw pictures in permanent places. Archaeologists have found paintings colored with yellow or red iron oxide and other mineral pigments, mostly showing animals, in caves used by the people of the Old Stone Age. Scientists do not believe that the people of this period lived in these caves, but they are not sure what the caves were used for. How do you think the Old Stone Age people might have used these caves? What significance do you think the paintings might have had?

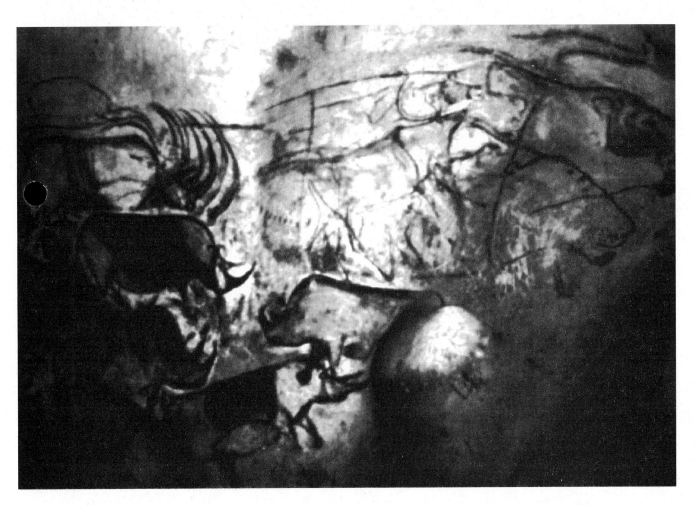

This painting is one of more than 300 discovered in early 1995 in a cave near Avignon, France. Since 1940 an average of one Old Stone Age cave has been found per year in southwestern Europe. Many more may lie under water but may never be discovered. The people of the Old Stone Age lived during the Ice Age. When Earth warmed at the end of the Ice Age, melting ice covered the land on which they lived with water.

Source: Robert Hughes, "Scenes from the Stone Age," *Time* (Vol. 145, February 13, 1995).

First Fruits of The Field

Kabyle Legend Retold by Anne Pellowski, 1990

Archaeologists know that sometime during the New Stone Age, people who once got their food only by hunting and gathering began to raise plants and animals to eat. This practice is called agriculture. Who first got the idea to grow their own food, and how did they get the idea? Nobody knows. So, people try to answer this question through stories known as legends. Many cultures pass down legends to explain events in nature and cultural traditions. Legends are often partially based on facts and are popularly believed to be true. The Kabyle people of northern Africa tell the following legend to explain how people learned to grow their own food. Why do you think the storyteller might have used an ant to teach the humans?

First Man and First Woman wandered around under the earth. One day they found a pile of wheat in a corner, and next to that a pile of barley. In other corners they found piles of seeds and grains of all kinds that are good to eat or to **season** food.

season: flavor

"What does this mean?" they wondered.

Near the wheat and barley ran an ant. First Parents saw the ant. It scratched the **hull** off a kernel of barley and then ate the grain inside.

hull: outer covering of a seed

"What are you doing?" First Parents asked the ant. "Can you tell us about these seeds and grains?"

The ant said, "Do you know of a spring or a pool or a river?"

First Parents said, "No, we do not know of such things. But we do know of a fountain."

The ant answered, "Then you do know Water. Water is there for you to drink. It is there for you to wash yourselves and your clothing. But Water is also there so that you can grow and cook your food. If you cook each of these grains, each in its own way, you will always have good food. Come with me. I want to show you."

The ant led First Parents to her passageway under the earth.

"This is my path. Come with me." The ant led First Parents up through the passageway and out onto the earth. She led them to a river and said, "Here flows much Water. You can use it to drink, and to wash yourselves and your clothing. And this is also the Water that you can use to cook your grains, after you have ground them up."

The ant led First Parents to a pair of stones and said, "We can use these stones to grind kernels into flour."

The ant helped First Man and First Woman grind some grains into flour. Then the ant showed them how to mix the flour with water, how to make a fire, and how to bake flat loaves of bread.

When they had eaten the bread until they were full, First Man said to First Woman, "Come, let us visit the earth." They took grains of wheat and barley and many other seeds. They wandered here and there. Often, they dropped a few kernels of grain or seeds. Rain fell on them and the kernels and seeds grew into plants.

When First Man and First Woman passed by on their return, they saw the plants, heavy with grain or seed pods. They dug into the earth and saw that each plant had grown from one grain or seed.

"In the future, we will eat half of the grain and plant the remaining half. We will wait until after the first rain falls."

This they did, and that is how the grains and seeds of plants were spread wider and wider, until they could be found growing over much of the earth.

The development of agriculture was a giant step in history. People no longer had to move from place to place in order to follow their food supply. They began to settle in one place and build communities. As people's farming techniques improved, not everyone had to be involved in the growing of food. New, specialized occupations developed. Some people continued to farm, while others ground grain into flour, and still others baked the bread. The development of agriculture changed civilization forever.

Source: Anne Pellowski, *Hidden Stories in Plants*. New York: Macmillan Publishing Co., 1990.

The Epic of Gilgamesh

Sumerian Epic, 3000–2000 B.C.

One of the oldest stories in the world is The Epic of Gilgamesh, *an ancient Sumerian tale that was written between 4,000 and 5,000 years ago. The story comes from Mesopotamia—in what is today the Middle East—and was originally carved on clay tablets. Gilgamesh was said to have been the king of Uruk, an ancient city in Mesopotamia, around 2700 B.C. In the epic Gilgamesh goes on a long journey in search of eternal youth and encounters monsters, gods, and the mighty forces of nature. In the excerpt below, a god tells Gilgamesh about a great flood that once swept the land. How does the god manage to survive the flood?*

For six days and six nights the winds blew, torrent and **tempest** and flood overwhelmed the world, tempest and flood raged together like warring hosts. When the seventh day dawned the storm from the south **subsided**, the sea grew calm, the flood was stilled; I looked at the face of the world and there was silence, all mankind was turned to clay. The surface of the sea stretched as flat as a roof-top; I opened a hatch and the light fell on my face. Then I bowed low, I sat down and I wept, the tears streamed down my face, for on every side was the waste of water. I looked for land in vain, but fourteen leagues distant there appeared a mountain, and there the boat grounded; on the mountain of Nisir the boat held fast, she held fast and did not budge. One day she held, and a second day on the mountain of Nisir she held fast and did not budge. A third day, and a fourth day she held fast on the mountain and did not budge; a fifth day and a sixth day she held fast on the mountain. When the seventh day dawned I loosed a dove and let her go. She flew away, but finding no resting-place she returned. Then I loosed a swallow, and she flew away but finding no resting-place she returned. I loosed a raven, she saw that the waters had retreated, she ate, she flew around, she **cawed**, and she did not come back. Then I threw everything open to the four winds, I made a sacrifice and poured out a **libation** on the mountain top.

tempest: storm

subsided: died down

cawed: squawked

libation: liquid offering

After telling this story, the god presents Gilgamesh with a plant that will give him eternal life. A serpent tricks him, however, causing Gilgamesh to lose the plant and the promise of eternal life. The Epic of Gilgamesh *is the oldest epic known to human history. Like* The Iliad *and the* Aeneid, *which you can read excerpts from on pages 30–32 and 38–39, it is considered one of the world's greatest works of literature.*

Source: N. K. Sandars, ed., *The Epic of Gilgamesh.* London: Penguin Group, 1960.

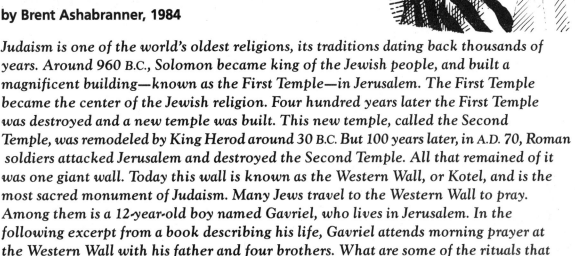

Praying at the Western Wall

by Brent Ashabranner, 1984

Judaism is one of the world's oldest religions, its traditions dating back thousands of years. Around 960 B.C., Solomon became king of the Jewish people, and built a magnificent building—known as the First Temple—in Jerusalem. The First Temple became the center of the Jewish religion. Four hundred years later the First Temple was destroyed and a new temple was built. This new temple, called the Second Temple, was remodeled by King Herod around 30 B.C. But 100 years later, in A.D. 70, Roman soldiers attacked Jerusalem and destroyed the Second Temple. All that remained of it was one giant wall. Today this wall is known as the Western Wall, or Kotel, and is the most sacred monument of Judaism. Many Jews travel to the Western Wall to pray. Among them is a 12-year-old boy named Gavriel, who lives in Jerusalem. In the following excerpt from a book describing his life, Gavriel attends morning prayer at the Western Wall with his father and four brothers. What are some of the rituals that Gavriel performs with his father? How do these rituals relate to Gavriel's religious beliefs?

*W*hen Abe and his sons go to morning prayer, the sun is just turning the eastern sky a rosy pink. Gavriel has learned from his father that morning prayer cannot be said until the light is just right. "Just enough to tell a light blue thread from a white one," Abe says. Gavriel rubs the sleep from his eyes as they walk to the Kotel, the Western Wall, but he does not wish that he were back in bed.

He has a special feeling for the Jewish quarter at this time of day, before the noise and bustle have really begun, before the narrow streets are crowded. He likes going to prayer with his father. He carries a blue velvet pouch which holds his father's prayer shawl and *tefillin*, which are small leather boxes containing Biblical verses.

They pass the rebuilt ruins of a **Crusader** lodging place and then walk down several flights of stone stairs—140 steps in all—to reach the Kotel. Morning is Gavriel's favorite time to come to the Western Wall. Some people are always there when they arrive but not so many as there will be later in the day. The sounds of prayer rise clearly in the cool, clean air. Swallows swoop overhead making little cries. It is a peaceful place to be.

Abe puts on his prayer shawl and the *tefillin*, which are provided with long leather straps. He places one of the *tefillin* on his left arm facing his heart and winds the leather strap around his left forearm seven times. The other *tefillin* he places in the center of his forehead, looping the leather strap around his head to keep the *tefillin* in place.

Crusader: name for Christian soldiers who fought from the 11th to 13th centuries to recapture Jerusalem from the Muslims

Gavriel knows the *tefillin* signify that the **covenant** with God is a matter of serious concern every day of the week. He remembers the passage from **Deuteronomy**: "And these words which I command thee this day shall be upon thine heart... And thou shalt bind them for thine hand, and they shall be for **frontlets** between thine eyes."

When the *tefillin* are properly attached, Abe begins to pray, and his sons join him. He has taught them the proper way of prayer just as he learned it from his father. They pray aloud, and Gavriel concentrates intently, not just saying words but thinking very hard about what they mean. This concentration, this thinking about what the prayer means, is called *kavvanah*, and it is of great importance. As with his father and other men in prayer at the Wall, the intensity of his concentration causes Gavriel's eyes to close and his body to sway.

"... O purify our hearts to serve Thee in truth, for Thou art God in truth, and Thy word is truth, and endureth forever...."

On many nights Abe helps Gavriel in his study of the **Talmud**. In just a few months Gavriel will become *bar mitzvah*, a son of the commandment. This will happen on the day he is thirteen years old. Then, in a religious sense, he will be a man and able to understand the commandments of the Torah and observe them on his own responsibility. Now it is Abe's responsibility to see that Gavriel really has that understanding.

Gavriel takes his religion seriously. Whenever he leaves the apartment or returns to it, he touches a piece of the **Torah**, called *mezuzah*, which has been nailed to the doorframe. He does the same with a piece of the Sacred Book that has been fastened to his classroom door at school.

And at family gatherings around the dinner table on the holy day of **Shabbat** or at **Passover**, when songs of praise and thanksgiving are sung, Gavriel's clear voice is loudest, after that of his father.

covenant: agreement

Deuteronomy: holy book of Jewish scripture

frontlets: decorated headbands

Talmud: Jewish law based on interpretations of sacred texts

Torah: Jewish scripture

Shabbat: Jewish sabbath from sundown Friday to sundown Saturday

Passover: Jewish holiday celebrating Exodus from Egypt

Today over 17 million people—or about 1 in 330 people in the world—are Jews. Judaism emerged in western Asia almost 4,000 years ago in what is today the nation of Israel. About 2,000 years ago another major religion—called Christianity—developed in the same region. To learn more about Christianity, read the document on pages 41–42.

Source: Brent Ashabranner, *Gavriel and Jemal: Two Boys of Jerusalem.* New York: Dodd, Mead & Company, 1984.

THE ROSETTA STONE

Egyptian Decree, 196 B.C.

For hundreds of years one of the world's greatest mysteries could be found on the walls of the pyramids and monuments of ancient Egypt. On these walls Egyptians had carved hieroglyphics, a system of writing that used pictures and signs to stand for objects, sounds, and ideas. At a later time Egyptians had carved another system of writing known as demotic, which used an alphabet to stand for sounds. What did these symbols mean? For years no one knew what they meant because the knowledge of how to read hieroglyphics and demotic writing had been lost.

But in 1799 archaeologists made a remarkable discovery. In the Egyptian town of Rosetta they found a piece of stone marked with carvings in three languages: hieroglyphics, demotic, and Greek. The Rosetta Stone appears in the inset on the facing page. Using their knowledge of Greek, scholars soon learned that the stone recorded the same information in the three different languages. The translation of the Rosetta Stone provided a valuable key for unlocking the secrets of ancient Egypt.

What did the markings on the Rosetta Stone say? It was an order given by a pharaoh named Ptolemy Epiphanes in 196 B.C., demanding that priests in Egypt honor him and accept him as their ruler. To make sure that everyone would obey this order, the pharaoh had it carved in three different languages.

Reading hieroglyphic symbols, or hieroglyphs, is like trying to solve a puzzle. Look at the sentence below taken from the Rosetta Stone. The meaning of each hieroglyph is given below it in English. Try to put the hieroglyphs together to make a sentence.

GOOD　EVERYTHING　HEALTH　STRENGTH　LIFE　MIGHT　VICTORY　THE GODS AND GODDESSES　GAVE HIM

This sentence appears on the facing page in the enlargement of the top right section of the Rosetta Stone. It is in the line beside the arrow. Can you find it? In English, this sentence reads: "The gods and goddesses have given him [Pharaoh] victory, might, strength, health, and every other good thing." You can use some of these symbols to decode other hieroglyphs as well. For example, you already know the symbol for life, which appears above. The symbol for eternal, shown below, is a snake. When these two symbols appear together, they mean eternal life. See if you can find this phrase on the next page. Notice that by combining symbols you can make longer phrases. Look at the symbols for day, seven, and ten. Now see if you can find the phrase 17 days on the Rosetta Stone. Try to locate the other symbols and phrases explained below. What do you suppose that the other hieroglyphs on the Rosetta Stone might mean?

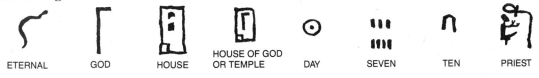

ETERNAL　GOD　HOUSE　HOUSE OF GOD OR TEMPLE　DAY　SEVEN　TEN　PRIEST

Thanks to the Rosetta Stone, people can now read hieroglyphic writing to learn about life in ancient Egypt. To find out about one of the most important Egyptian leaders in history, read the next document on page 17.

Hatshepsut, His Majesty, Herself

by Catherine M. Andronik

Hatshepsut (hat SHEP soot), (1520–1482 B.C.), was the best known and most powerful female pharaoh of ancient Egypt. She came to the throne in 1503 B.C., after the death of her husband, Tuthmosis II. Since her stepson, Tuthmosis III, was too young to assume the responsibilities of being pharaoh, Hatshepsut was appointed to rule Egypt as a regent until he could assume the throne. Later, she had herself crowned pharaoh and ruled until her death in 1482 B.C. During Hatshepsut's reign Egypt enjoyed peace and prosperity, expanding its trade with East Africa and Asia. She built a lavish temple at Deir el-Bahri to keep her name alive. Her life story, including the major achievements of her reign, were recorded in beautiful carvings and paintings on the temple walls. As you read this excerpt from her biography, think about the characteristics that enabled Hatshepsut to become a successful ruler. What kind of decisions did she have to make? Why do you think her power and influence grew? How do you think her stepson felt about her?

Hatshepsut's father, Pharaoh Tuthmosis I, died at the relatively old age of fifty. His secret tomb, the first underground chamber to be hidden in the towering cliffs of the Valley of the Kings, just northwest of Thebes, had been excavated in advance. The fine sarcophagus, or stone coffin, which would hold his body was also ready. The pharaoh's mummy was carefully prepared, as befitted a great and beloved king. After seventy days, with solemn ceremony, Tuthmosis was laid in a tomb filled with all the choice food and drink, games and furniture, clothing and jewelry, and the little clay servant figures, called shawabtis (shah-WAHB-tees), that he could possibly need in the afterlife.

Following her father's death, Hatshepsut married her half brother, and the young man was crowned Pharaoh Tuthmosis II. Hatshepsut may have been only about twelve years old. As queen, she received a variety of new titles. Her favorite was God's Wife. Tuthmosis II and Hatshepsut had one child, a daughter named Neferure (neh-feh-ROO-ray).

The reign of Tuthmosis II was unremarkable. It was also brief, for he was a sickly young man. Within a few years of his coronation, Hatshepsut's husband had died.

With the death of Tuthmosis II, Egypt was left without a king to ensure that the many gods would look kindly upon the fragile desert land. *Maat* [cosmic order] was a delicate thing, and without a pharaoh to tend to its preservation, it was in danger of collapsing.

Although Hatshepsut had been Tuthmosis II's Great Wife, he'd had other wives in his harem, including one named Isis. Isis had borne the pharaoh a baby boy, who was also named Tuthmosis. Since Isis was not royal, neither was her baby. But like his father, he could grow up to be pharaoh if he married a princess of the royal blood: his half sister, Neferure.

Until Tuthmosis III was mature enough to be crowned pharaoh what Egypt needed was a regent, an adult who could take control of the country. The regent would have to be someone familiar with palace life and **protocol.** He would need to conduct himself with the proper authority around the royal advisors. He should be prepared to wield power if it became necessary, and he should feel comfortable around visiting dignitaries from other lands. He needed to know his place among the priests of the various gods.

It was a job Hatshepsut, perhaps just fifteen years old, had been training for since her earliest days by her father's side. Women had acted as regents for infants at other times in Egypt's history, and the gods had not frowned upon them.

So until Tuthmosis III was ready to be crowned as pharaoh, the acting ruler of Egypt would be his aunt, the royal widow of the king, Hatshepsut.

At first, little Tuthmosis III was considered the pharaoh, with Hatshepsut just his second-in-command. But a small child could not be an **effective** ruler. As Hatshepsut settled into her role as regent, she gradually took on more and more of the royal decision-making. She appointed officials and advisors; dealt with the priests; appeared in public ceremonies first behind, then beside, and eventually in front of her nephew. Gradually, over seven years, her power and influence grew. In the end, Hatshepsut was ruling Egypt in all but name.

There is no reliable record of exactly when or how it happened, but at some point Hatshepsut took a bold and **unprecedented** step: She had herself crowned pharaoh with the large, heavy, red-and-white double crown of the two Egypts, north and south. Since all pharaohs took a throne name, a sort of symbolic name, upon their **coronation,** Hatshepsut chose Maatkare (math-KAH-ray). *Maat,* that crucial cosmic order, was important to Hatshepsut. Egypt required a strong pharaoh to ensure *maat.* Hatshepsut could be that pharaoh—even if she did happen to be a woman.

A few women had tried to rule Egypt before, but never with such a valid claim to the throne or at such a time of peace and prosperity. When Queens Nitocris and Sobekneferu had come to the throne in earlier dynasties, Egypt had been suffering from political problems, and there had been no male heirs. These women had not ruled long or well, and neither had had the audacity to proclaim herself pharaoh. Hatshepsut would be different.

There was no word in the language of Egypt for a female ruler; a queen was simply the wife of a king. Hatshepsut had no choice: she had to call herself pharaoh, or king—a male title. She was concerned with preserving and continuing traditional order as much as possible, so to the people of Egypt she made herself look like a man in her role as pharaoh. In ceremonies, she wore a man's short kilt instead of a woman's long dress, much as she had as a child. Around her neck she wore a king's broad collar. She even fastened a false golden beard to her chin. When she wrote about herself as pharaoh, sometimes she referred to herself as he, other times as she. This would be very confusing to historians trying to uncover her identity thousands of years later.

Since Hatshepsut could not marry a queen, her daughter Neferure acted as God's Wife in public rituals. It was good training for Neferure, who would in time be expected to marry her half brother, Tuthmosis III, and be his royal **consort**. But Hatshepsut never seems to have considered that her daughter could succeed her as pharaoh.

consort: a spouse

Hatshepsut might have had to look and act like a man in public, but she never gave up feminine pleasures. Archaeologists have uncovered bracelets and alabaster cosmetic pots with Hatshepsut's cartouche (kar-TOOSH), or hieroglyphic name symbol, inscribed on each. Both men and women in Egypt used cosmetics. They needed creams and oils to keep their skin and hair from drying out under the brutal desert sun. And the kohl, a kind of makeup made from powdered lead that people applied around their eyes, did more than make them attractive; it also helped block out the sun's glare. But Hatshepsut was especially particular about her appearance. One inscription describes her as "more beautiful than anything."

After Hatshepsut's death, her stepson, Tuthmosis III became pharaoh. He vengefully destroyed much of her great memorial; however, the ruins of this magnificent temple still survive and can be seen by visitors.

Source: Catherine M. Andronik, *Hatshepsut, His Majesty, Herself.* New York: Atheneum Books for Young Readers, 2001.

Howard Carter's Diary

by Howard Carter

Howard Carter (1874–1939), was a British archaeologist, who is best known for his discovery of the tomb of Tutankhamen (too tahng KAH mun), who ruled Egypt from about 1347 B.C. until his death in 1339 B.C. The pharaoh was entombed in the Valley of the Kings, a burial center at Thebes, the Egyptian capital. The ancient Egyptians believed in a life after death and were buried with their favorite possessions for later use in the after-life. According to custom, the young pharaoh, who died before he was twenty, was buried with all his belongings. Most of the pharaohs' tombs in the ancient burial center had been found and looted by robbers, who stole many valuable treasures. However, Carter and his employer, Lord Carnarvon, knew that King Tut's tomb had not yet been discovered. After searching the area unsuccessfully for about ten years, Carter finally achieved his goal. In November of 1922, the entrance to the tomb, which had been covered in rubble for centuries, was cleared. The four rooms of the royal tomb had kept their secrets for 3,300 years. The discovery was significant because the tomb had not been opened since ancient times and was largely intact. Carter and his team were stunned by the discovery of more than 5,000 objects, including thrones, beds, clothing, chariots, and jewelry. One of the most famous treasures from the tomb is a lifelike gold mask of Tutankhamen, which covered the head and shoulders of the royal mummy. As you read this selection, think about Howard Carter's thoughts when he first looked inside the tomb. What do you think it was like to discover how the ancient pharaohs had lived?

Gradually the scene grew clearer, and we could pick out individual objects. First, right opposite to us—we had been conscious of them all the while, but refused to believe in them—were three great **gilt** couches, their sides carved in the form of monstrous animals, curiously **attenuated** in body, as they had to be to serve their purpose, but with heads of startling realism. Uncanny beasts enough to look upon at any time: seen as we saw them, their brilliant gilded surfaces picked out of the darkness by our electric torch, as though by limelight, their heads throwing grotesque distorted shadows on the wall behind them, they were almost terrifying. Next, on the right, two statues caught and held our attention: two life-sized figures of a king in black, facing each other like sentinels, gold kilted, gold sandalled, armed with mace and staff, the protective sacred cobra upon their foreheads.

gilt: to overlay with a thin covering of gold
attenuated: weakened, reduced in severity

These were the dominant objects that caught the eye at first. Between them, around them, piled on top of them, there were countless others—exquisitely painted and **inlaid** caskets; **alabaster** vases, some beautifully carved in openwork designs; strange black shrines, from the open door of one a great gilt snake peeping out; bouquets of flowers or leaves; beds; chairs beautifully carved; a golden inlaid throne; a heap of curious white **oviform** boxes; **staves** of all shapes and designs; beneath our eyes, on the very threshold of the chamber, a beautiful **lotiform** cup of **translucent** alabaster; on the left a confused pile of overturned chariots, glistening with gold and inlay; and peeping from behind them another portrait of a king.

Such were some of the objects that lay before us. Whether we noted them all at the time I cannot say for certain, as our minds were in much too excited and confused a state to register accurately. Presently it dawned upon our bewildered brains that in all this medley of objects before us there was no coffin or trace of mummy, and the much-debated question of tomb or **cache** began to intrigue us afresh. With this question in view we re-examined the scene before us, and noticed for the first time that between the two black sentinel statues on the right there was another sealed doorway. The explanation gradually dawned upon us. We were but on the threshold of our discovery. What we saw was merely an **antechamber.** Behind the guarded door there were to be other chambers, possibly a succession of them, and in one of them, beyond any shadow of doubt, we should find the Pharaoh lying.

We had seen enough, and our brains began to reel at the thought of the task in front of us. We reclosed the hole, locked the wooden grille that had been placed in the first doorway, left our native staff on guard, mounted our donkeys and rode home down The Valley, strangely silent and subdued.

The discovery of the tomb of King Tutankhamen enabled archaeologists to learn more about an ancient society that had produced great artists, engineers, and architects. Today, visitors to the Cairo Museum in Egypt can see most of the items found in the tomb on display.

Source: Raymond Holden, *Famous Scientific Expeditions.* New York: Random House, Inc., 1955

---

inlaid: set into a surface in a decorative design
alabaster: white and translucent gypsum carved into vases

oviform: shaped like an egg
staves: strips of wood or narrow iron plates used to form the sides of a structure.
lotiform: a small, spherical bowl for holding water
translucent: clear, transparent

cache: hiding place

antechamber: an outer room

Life of a Hindu Priest

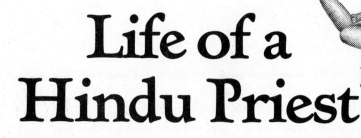

NATARAJ

by Hardwari Lal, 1984

About 4,000 years ago, the religion of Hinduism begin to develop on the subcontinent of India. Hinduism developed from ancient beliefs and stories. Hindus believe in many different gods. Some of these gods are pictured in the illustrations accompanying this selection. Hindus also believe that all parts of nature are holy. Hardwari Lal is a 55-year-old Hindu pandit, or priest, who works at a temple in Bhatinda, a town in northern India near the Pakistani border. As you read Hardwari Lal's description of his duties in a selection from an oral history, think about how the rituals he and other Hindus perform relate to their religious beliefs.

My day at the temple begins at half-past four in the morning and ends at eight o'clock every night. It's a long day, but I don't mind one bit, as I devote all the time to the service of God.

Which God, you ask? Well, we Hindus have 330 million **deities**. We believe that the God Brahma is the Creator of the World. Vishnu is the God who preserves the world and the God Shiva is the destroyer of the world.

deities: gods

Among the more popular gods and goddesses are Radha and Krishna, Ram and Sita, Hanuman the monkey god, Ganesha the elephant-headed god, and the Goddess Durga, who rides a tiger. We have lots of **idols** of these gods and goddesses in our temple. You'll find lots of temples in India, at least one every mile or so, for religion is very important here.

idols: statues

It's part of my duty as a priest to offer prayer to the idols, to bathe them with milk and honey, and to dress them. Then, every day, other temple priests and I have to organize the distribution of free food. Our temple feeds about thirty or forty poor people every day. The temple gets its money from donations.

Only a **Brahman** can become a priest in a temple. He must be learned in the ancient Sanskrit texts known as *Vedas*. He must also know how to conduct weddings, birth and death ceremonies, and so on.

Brahman: member of the Hindu priest class

Most marriages are finally arranged after comparing the horoscopes of the boy and girl. If the astrologer feels that they will get along, he fixes an **auspicious** day and hour for the wedding. Last year, for almost eight months, practically no weddings took place, as the stars weren't in the right position.

auspicious: lucky

Anyhow, on the chosen day, the bridegroom dresses in style with a shining crown on his head and **garlands** of flowers and **rupees** round his neck. He then sits on a white horse—though some people prefer automobiles nowadays. Escorted by a band of drummers and trumpeters and a whole lot of relatives and friends, the groom goes through the streets to the bride's home. The bride has to wear lots of jewelry and dress in red or pink.

garlands: wreaths
rupees: Indian coins

The priests light the sacred fire of sandalwood and incense and begin reciting **mantras** from the *Vedas*. Then we take a pink cloth and tie one end to the bridegroom and the other end to the bride. The bride and bridegroom have to walk around the sacred fire seven times to become husband and wife. For tens of centuries, Hindu weddings have been performed in the same way.

mantras: prayers

As for funerals, we Hindus usually burn our dead, though we bury infants.

There are so many holy cities and places. They're usually on the banks of rivers or up on the snowy mountains. Cities like Hardwar, Rishikesh and Varanasi are on the riverside. Pilgrimage centers like Badrinath, Kedarnath and Amarnath are high up in the mountains. Half the year the pilgrims can't get to them because of the snow.

But I must tell you about the Kumbh *Mela*, which is held every twelve years and is the world's greatest religious fair. At Kumbh, millions and millions of Hindus gather from all over India to take a bath in the holy Ganges [River].

With so much going on, life remains busy and full for me. I can't tell you how happy and fortunate I feel serving God and the people.

SHIVA   PARVATI

KRISHNA

RAMA   SITA

Today nearly 800 million people—or about one in seven people in the world—are Hindus. Most Hindus live in India and Southeast Asia. Around 2,500 years ago a Hindu prince founded another major religion of the world. To learn about this religion, read the document on pages 24–25.

Source: Veenu Sanal, *We Live in India.* New York: The Bookwright Press, 1984.

Becoming a Buddhist Master

by Sek Bao Shi, 1985

Around 563 B.C. a Hindu prince named Siddhartha Gautama was born in the foothills of the Himalaya Mountains in what is today Nepal. After trying for years to understand suffering and find widsom, Siddhartha decided that suffering was caused by desires. By freeing himself of desires, Siddhartha said he reached peace and was free of pain and suffering. When he told his followers what he had learned, they began to call him the Buddha, a title meaning "the Awakened One." From Siddhartha's teachings a new religion called Buddhism developed and spread throughout Southeast Asia. Sek Bao Shi was a 41-year-old resident of Singapore who was working toward becoming a Buddhist master. As you read this account of her life from an oral history, notice the different rituals and practices that she follows. How do her Buddhist beliefs shape her life?

It's 4:30 A.M. The sky is dark and it's rather cold, but I'm up and so are the other five members of our Buddhist Order. Only women live in our temple. By 5:00 A.M. we're chanting Buddhist **sutras** at our first service of the day.

sutras: teachings, scriptures

At 7:00 A.M. we make our first offering of biscuits or bread and a cup of tea to Lord Buddha. A short service accompanies the offering.

24

Then we have our breakfast of bread or oatmeal and a hot drink. We are **vegetarians**, because we don't believe in harming any living creature.

After breakfast, there are chores to do. These include cleaning, washing and preparing lunch. At 11:00 A.M., after the rice is cooked, we make a second offering to Lord Buddha. We have our lunch soon after and this is the final meal of the day.

To become a member of the Buddhist Order, it's customary to follow a Master or *Shi Fu* of one's choice for five years. When I decided to leave home, give up my job, rid myself of my worldly possessions, shave my head and devote myself to practicing Lord Buddha's teachings, I asked to be her **disciple**. I was very happy to be accepted. I have been my *Shi Fu's* disciple for three years now.

My decision to join the Buddhist Order was not made overnight. I had been thinking about it since I was 9. As a child, I often accompanied my mother, a devout Buddhist, to the Kuan Yin Temple to make offerings to Kuan Yin, the Goddess of Mercy.

After completing my secondary schooling, I entered the civil service. Still deeply interested in the teachings of Lord Buddha, I became a vegetarian. As a lay devotee I went to the Buddhist Union Shrine to help out in religious and administrative activities. I also resolved to abstain from harming others, from stealing, from telling lies, from being unchaste and from all forms of intoxicating drinks and drugs. I spent seventeen years in this way until finally deciding to join the Buddhist Order at the age of 38.

Since then, I have been staying at the Leng Jin Temple to study the Buddhist scriptures with my *Shi Fu*. In addition, she teaches me how to **meditate**, conduct Buddhist services and beat the drum and cymbals during special ceremonies. I also have more than 500 rules to observe now.

I've found peace and happiness in the teachings of our Lord Buddha who said, "The gift of Truth excels all other gifts." I want to seek this Truth through the study of the Buddhist scriptures. I know it can be found within ourselves.

I am glad for the opportunity to practice what I believe in. There's complete freedom of worship in Singapore and wherever you go you will see temples, mosques, churches and other places of worship near to each other.

As a Buddhist, I'm very happy to see our people understanding and accepting one another's customs and religion. It makes for a much happier world.

Today more than 330 million people—or about 1 in 17 people in the world—are Buddhists. Buddhism, along with Judaism, Christianity, Islam, and Hinduism, all began in Asia. Over the course of hundreds of years, these five religions have spread to every part of the world. They have had an enormous impact on both world civilization and history.

vegetarians: people who do not eat meat

disciple: follower

meditate: focus one's thoughts

Source: Jessie Wee, *We Live in Malaysia & Singapore*. New York: The Bookwright Press, 1985.

25

The Terra Cotta Army of Emperor Qin

by Caroline Lazo

Imagine traveling back in time more than 2,000 years to ancient China and gazing in wonder at giant figures made for the famous tomb site of the First Emperor. That's exactly what happened to some modern-day Chinese farmers who accidentally uncovered the terra cotta, or clay, figures in a wheat field. These life-size statues of soldiers form a terra cotta army that was made to guard the emperor after he died. Amazingly, each figure is so realistic that scientists think they were made to look like actual soldiers in the emperor's army. Some of the figures seem about to smile in greeting, while others glare angrily, warning intruders to keep away. The soldiers even carry real weapons, which are as sharp today as when they were first buried. As you read this selection, think about what it would be like to study these statues. How could this discovery help archeologists learn more about Chinese history and art?

Ying Zheng was only 13 years old when he became King of Qin, the largest of the warring states in China. (Qin is pronounced *Chin*, and is the origin of the word *China*.) As soon as he was crowned, the young king made plans for the construction of his tomb, because he knew it would take a lifetime to build. After he unified China in 221 B.C. and proclaimed himself First Emperor, full-scale work began on the immense tomb complex, which scholars now call "one of the most extraordinary memorials on earth" and "the greatest archaeological find of out time."

Details of the tomb's scale and contents had been described in ancient folktales too bizarre for modern scholars to believe. In the Shiji (ancient historical records), facts about the First Emperor's tomb come to life:

More than 700,000 workers from all parts of China labored there. They dug through the underground streams; poured molten copper for the outer coffin; and they filled the burial chamber with models of palaces, towers and official buildings, as well as fine utensils, precious stones and rarities. **Artisans** *were ordered to fix automatic crossbows so that grave robbers would be slain. The waterways of the empire, the Yellow and Yang-tzu Rivers. . . . were represented by mercury and were made to flow mechanically. Above, the heavenly constellations were depicted. . . . An official suggested that the artisans responsible for mechanical devices knew too much about the contents of the tomb for safety. Therefore, once the First Emperor was placed in the burial chamber and the treasures sealed up, the middle and outer gates were shut to imprison all those who had worked on the tomb. No one came out. Trees and grass were then planted over the* **mausoleum** *to make it look like a hill.*

artisans: skilled workers

mausoleum: a large tomb

Rivers of mercury flowing underground? Models of palaces, towers, and buildings encased below the earth? Could such tales be true? For centuries the stories spread throughout China and aroused people's interest. But no matter how curious they were, the Chinese wouldn't dream of disturbing a tomb; such an act would have been a **sacrilege** and a crime. But opinions changed, and by the 20th century, the government viewed certain burial places as vivid examples of China's heritage and as valuable tools in the education of its people.

sacrilege: irreverence toward a holy place or thing

Also, modern land development began to threaten sacred sites camouflaged for centuries by grass and trees. Sometimes archaeologists have had to work fast to beat developers to the sites, not because they are opposed to new building, but because they are dedicated to preserving the beauty as well as the lessons of China's past,

No one would have guessed that a simple accident in a wheat field would lead to the discovery of the most elaborate tomb site of all. But it did.

In March 1974 farmers digging a well in a field near the city of Xian in Central China were surprised when their shovels struck a hard object 14 feet underground. They guessed it was a pottery vessel of some kind, because the tip of it was the reddish brown color of clay. But they were even more surprised, when, trying to free it from the earth, they found a perfectly sculpted head of a soldier instead! Digging deeper, a life-size figure—over six feet tall—began to appear.

The farmers reported their unique find, and soon archaeologists came to the scene and continued to dig. One after another, clay figures emerged from the earth, still standing in formation 20 feet below the ground.

Further excavation confirmed what no one had dared to imagine: The farmers had actually uncovered the legendary army assigned to guard the First Emperor in the afterlife, just as the ancient folktales had described.

"The remarkable quality of the statues stunned us all," said Robert Jacobsen, a member of the first group of Americans invited to Xian, "and the size of the site—comparable in area to Cambridge, England—still boggles the mind." As more and more warriors emerged from the ground, it became clear that the mound where the tomb itself was located was just the tip of the iceberg, and that the tomb's contents could someday rival those of the tomb of Egypt's Tutankhamen. But it will be many years before archaeologists reach the actual tomb, because thousands of clay soldiers—whole formations—must be repaired and restored along the way.

Although the tomb site was first discovered in 1974, it was several years before the Chinese leaders allowed people from other countries to see it.

Source: Caroline Lazo, *The Terra Cotta Army of Emperor Qin*. New York: Macmillan Publishing, 1993.

A Letter from a Han Emperor

by Emperor Wen Ti, about 160 B.C.

Around 200 B.C. China's emperor, Shihuangdi (SHEE hwahng dee), ordered the connection and strengthening of the walls along the northern border of the empire. These walls, like the Great Wall built many centuries later, served as a division from and protection against the people of the northern steppes. In spite of these walls, however, the Chinese sometimes had conflicts with their northern neighbors. The following excerpt is from a letter written by the Han emperor Wen Ti, who ruled China from 179–157 B.C. The letter was sent to the Captain, the leader of the Hsiung-nu (SYUNG NOO) people of the northern steppes. What cultural differences does Wen Ti mention in his letter? Do Wen Ti and the leader of the Hsiung-nu seek a peaceful resolution to their conflict?

We respectfully trust that the great Captain is well. We have respectfully received the two horses which the great Captain forwarded to Us.

The first Emperor of this dynasty adopted the following policy:— All to the north of the Long Wall, comprising the nations of the bow and arrow, to be **subject to** the great Captain: all within the Long Wall—namely, the **families of the hat and girdle**, to be subject to the House of Han. Thus, these peoples would each pursue their own **avocations**,—Ours, agriculture and manufacture of cloth; yours, archery and hunting,—in the acquisition of food and **raiment**. Father and son would not suffer separation; **suzerain** and **vassal** would rest in peace; and neither side would do violence to the other.

But of late We hear that certain worthless persons have been **incited** by the hope of gain to shake off their natural allegiance. **Breaches of** moral obligation and of treaty have occurred. There has been forgetfulness of family ties; and the tranquility of suzerain and vassal is at an end. This, however, belongs to the past. Your letter says, "The two States had become friendly; their rulers friends. The tramp of armies had been stilled for more peaceful occupations, and great joy had come upon successive generations at the new order of things." We truly rejoice over these words. Let us then **tread** together this path of wisdom in due compassion for the peoples committed to our charge. Let us make a fresh start. Let us secure quiet to the aged; and to the young, opportunity to grow up, and, without risk of harm, to **complete their allotted span**.

subject to: ruled by

families of the hat and girdle: people of the Han empire

avocations: occupations

raiment: clothing

suzerain: high-ranking, wealthy noble

vassal: lesser noble

incited: moved to action

Breaches of: breaks in

tread: walk

complete their allotted span: live out their lives

Like many other world leaders, both past and present, Emperor Wen Ti and the Captain worked together to achieve peace, despite their peoples' differences.

Source: Hanscom, Hellerman and Posner, eds., *Voices of the Past: Readings in Ancient History.* The Macmillan Company, 1967.

THE ANCIENT WORLD

*For several days before the eruption
there had been earth tremors,
which had not caused much alarm,
since they often happen in the
Naples area. But that night they
were so strong that they not merely
shook but overturned everything.*

Pliny the Younger, A.D. 79

The Iliad

by Homer, about the 700s B.C.

More than 3,000 years ago, a rich civilization flourished in ancient Greece. Theater and poetry played an important role in Greek life. The Greeks often gathered at festivals to watch plays and to hear epics, or long poems, that celebrated their history and their many gods and goddesses. The earliest of the Greek poets whose works still survive is Homer, who probably lived between the 9th and 7th centuries B.C. One of Homer's greatest epics, The Iliad, *tells about the Trojan War, which Greece fought against Troy in the 12th century B.C. In the excerpt below, the Greek hero Achilles has just learned that his best friend Patroklos has died in battle. What role do Greek gods and goddesses play in* The Iliad?

Achilles' goddess-mother heard the sound of his grief as she sat within the depths of the Ocean. She came to him as he was still moaning terribly. She took his hand and clasped it and said, "My child, **why weep'st thou?**" Achilles ceased his moaning and answered, "Patroklos, my dear friend, has been **slain**. Now I shall have no joy in my life save the joy of **slaying** Hector who slew my friend."

Thetis, his goddess-mother, wept when she heard such speech from Achilles. "Shortlived you will be, my son," she said, "for it is **appointed** by the gods that after the death of Hector your death will come."

'**Straightway** then let me die," said Achilles, "since I let my friend die without giving him help. . . . Here I stayed, a useless **burthen** on the earth, while my comrades and my own dear friend fought for their country—here I stayed, I who am the best of all the Greeks. But now let me go into the battle and let the Trojans know that Achilles has come back, although he **tarried** long."

why weep'st thou:
  why do you cry?

slain: killed
slaying: killing

appointed: decided

straightway:
  immediately
burthen: burden

tarried: waited

"But **thine** armor, my son," said Thetis. "Thou hast no armor now to protect thee in the battle. Go not into it until thou seest me again. In the morning I shall return and I shall bring thee armor that **Hephaistos**, the **smith** of the gods, shall make for thee."

So she spoke, and she turned from her son, and she went to Olympus where the gods have their **dwellings**. . . .

Now Thetis, the mother of Achilles, went to Olympus where the gods have their dwellings and to the house of Hephaistos, the smith of the gods. That house shone above all the houses on Olympus because Hephaistos himself had made it of shining bronze. . . .

Hephaistos was lame and crooked of foot and went limping. He and Thetis were friends from of old time, for, when his mother would have **forsaken** him because of his crooked foot, Thetis and her sister **reared** him within one of the Ocean's caves and it was while he was with them that he began to work in metals. So the lame god was pleased to see Thetis in his dwelling and he welcomed her and clasped her hand and asked of her what she would have him do for her.

Then Thetis, weeping, told him of her son Achilles, how he had lost his dear friend and how he was moved to go into the battle to fight with Hector, and how he was without armor to protect his life, seeing that the armor that the gods had once given his father was now in the hands of his foe. And Thetis **besought** Hephaistos to make new armor for her son that he might go into the battle.

She no sooner finished speaking than Hephaistos went to his workbench. . . .

For the armor of Achilles he made first a shield and then a **corselet** that gleamed like fire. And he made a strong helmet to go on the head and shining **greaves** to wear on the ankles. The shield was made with five folds, one fold of metal upon the other, so that it was so strong and thick that no spear or arrow could pierce it. And upon this shield he hammered out images that were a wonder to men. . . .

Not long was he in making the shield and the other wonderful pieces of armor. As soon as the armor was ready Thetis put her hands upon it, and flying down from Olympus like a hawk, brought it to the feet of Achilles, her son. . . .

Then Achilles put his shining armor upon him and it fitted him as though it were wings; he put the wonderful shield before him and he took in his hands the great spear that Cheiron the **Centaur** had given to Peleus his father—that spear that no one else but Achilles could wield. He bade his **charioteer** harness the **immortal** horses Xanthos and Balios. Then as he mounted his chariot Achilles spoke to the horses. "Xanthos and Balios," he said, "this time bring the hero that goes with you back safely to the ships, and do not leave him dead on the plain as **ye** left the hero Patroklos."

Then Xanthos the immortal **steed** spoke, answering for himself and his comrade. "Achilles," he said, with his head bowed and his mane touching the ground, "Achilles, for this time we will bring thee safely

thine: your

Hephaistos: Greek god of fire

smith: one who makes metal objects

dwellings: homes

forsaken: abandoned

reared: raised

besought: begged

corselet: armor for the upper body

greaves: armor for the leg below the knee

centaur: creature that is half-human, half-horse

charioteer: driver of a chariot, or carriage

immortal: godlike

ye: you

steed: horse

back from the battle. But a day will come when we shall not bring thee back, when thou too shalt lie with the dead before the walls of Troy."

Then was Achilles troubled and he said, "Xanthos, my steed, why dost thou remind me by thy **prophecies** of what I know already—that my death too is appointed, and that I am to **perish** here, far from my father and my mother and my own land."

Then he drove his immortal horses into the battle. The Trojans were **affrighted** when they saw Achilles himself in the fight, blazing in the armor that Hephaistos had made for him. They went backward before his **onset**. And Achilles shouted to the captains of the Greeks, "No longer stand apart from the men of Troy, but go with me into the battle and let each man throw his whole soul into the fight."

And on the Trojan side Hector cried to his captains and said, "Do not let Achilles drive you before him. Even though his hands are as irresistible as fire and his fierceness as terrible as flashing steel, I shall go against him and face him with my spear." . . .

And when Achilles saw Hector before him he cried out, "Here is the man who most deeply wounded my soul, who slew my dear friend Patroklos. Now shall we two fight each other and Patroklos shall be **avenged** by me." And he shouted to Hector, "Now Hector, the day of thy triumph and the day of thy life is at its end."

But Hector answered him without fear, "Not with words, Achilles, can you affright me. Yet I know that thou art a man of might and a stronger man than I. But the fight between us depends upon the will of the gods. I shall do my best against thee, and my spear before this has been found to have a dangerous edge."

He spoke and lifted up his spear and flung it at Achilles. Then the breath of a god turned Hector's spear aside, for it was not appointed that either he or Achilles should be then slain. Achilles darted at Hector to slay him with his spear. But a god hid Hector from Achilles in a thick mist. . . .

Then on toward the City, [Achilles] went like a fire raging through a **glen** that had been **parched** with heat. Now on a tower of the walls of Troy, Priam the old King stood, and he saw the Trojans coming in a **rout** toward the City, and he saw Achilles in his armor blazing like a star—like that star that is seen at harvest time and is called Orion's Dog; the star that is the brightest of all stars, but yet is a sign of evil. And the old man Priam sorrowed greatly as he stood upon the tower and watched Achilles, because he knew in his heart whom this man would slay—Hector, his son, the protector of his City.

prophecies: predictions

perish: die

affrighted: frightened

onset: attack

avenged: revenged

glen: valley
parched: burned dry
rout: retreat

In a later battle Achilles killed the Trojan leader Hector. But, just as the gods had predicted, Achilles was also killed in battle, the result of a wound from a Trojan arrow. After many long years of warfare, the Greeks finally defeated the Trojans. For hundreds of years, the Greeks retold the story of the battles, gods, and heroes described in The Iliad. *Today this epic poem remains one of the greatest works of literature ever written.*

Source: Padraic Colum, *The Children's Homer*. New York: Macmillan Publishing Company, 1982.

The Birds

by Aristophanes, 414 B.C.

The ancient Greeks often held celebrations, or festivals. Plays, both funny and serious, were an important part of these festivals. Aristophanes (ar uh STOF uh neez) (about 450–388 B.C.) was an Athenian writer famous for his comedies. He was an expert in a special kind of comedy, called satire, that uses humor to criticize people and their actions. Those who attended a performance of The Birds in Aristophanes' day would have recognized the bird characters as people, sometimes important government leaders of Athens. Why might Aristophanes have disguised his characters as birds? In The Birds, Aristophanes was protesting Athens's war with Sicily. A peace seeker, Pisthetairos (pihs tay TĪ rohs), persuades the birds (who stand for ideal Athenians) to build a perfect walled city in the sky between Heaven and Earth. The birds (Athenians) could get over the wall, but humans (Sicilians) could not. What images come to mind as you read this excerpt describing how the wall was built?

SCENE

[*Reenter* PISTHETAIROS *with his attendants*]

PISTHETAIROS: The **omens** are favorable, I'm glad to say. Strange that we've had no news about the wall.—But here comes a messenger now, puffing like an Olympic sprinter.

[*Enter* FIRST MESSENGER, *wildly*]

MESSENGER: Where is he? Where is he? Where is he?

PISTHETAIROS: Where is who?

MESSENGER: The Chief. Pisthetairos.

PISTHETAIROS: Here.

MESSENGER: Great news! Great news! Your Wall is finished!

PISTHETAIROS: That *is* great news.

MESSENGER: Oh how shall I describe the splendor of that Wall, the [incredible] hugeness? Take two chariots, hitch four fat Wooden Horses to each one, let [two drivers] meet head-on—, they'd pass each other without a scratch. It's that big.

omens: signs from the gods and goddesses

33

PISTHETAIROS: Holy **Heraklês**!

MESSENGER: And tall? Look, I measured it myself: it stands six hundred feet!

PISTHETAIROS: Merciful **Poseidon**! What workmen could build a wall as high as that?

MESSENGER: Birds, only birds. Not a single Egyptian **hodcarrier** or stonemason or carpenter in the gang; birds did it all, and my eyes are popping yet. Imagine thirty thousand Cranes from **Libya**, each one with a belly full of stones for the **Rails** to shape up with their beaks; ten thousand Storks, at least, all of them making bricks with clay and water flown up by **Curlews** from the earth below.

PISTHETAIROS: **Mortar**?

PISTHETAIROS: **Herons** with **hods**.

PISTHETAIROS: How did they manage it?

MESSENGER: *That* was a triumph of technology! The Geese shoveled it up with their big feet.

PISTHETAIROS: Ah feet, to what use can **ye** not be put!

MESSENGER: Why, good Lord! There were Ducks to set the bricks, and flights of little apprentice Swallows with **trowel** tails for the mortar in their bills.

PISTHETAIROS: Who wants hired labor after this?—But the **joists** and beams?

MESSENGER: All handled by birds. When the Woodpeckers went to work on those **portals** it sounded like a shipyard!—So there's your Wall, complete with gates and locks, watchfires burning, patrols circling, the guard changed every hour. But I must wash off this long trek of mine. You'll know what to do next.

[*Exit* FIRST MESSENGER]

KORYPHAIOS (kor IHF ī ohs): Surprises you, hey? That quick job on your Wall?

PISTHETAIROS: Surprises me? Why, it's a lie come true!

The wall blocks the people of Sicily from communicating with their gods and makes them surrender. The play ends with a victory for the Athenians. Aristophanes wrote 55 plays altogether. Eleven of them have survived and are still performed today. One of them, **The Clouds,** *makes fun of the philosopher Socrates.*

Source: Dudley Fitts, translator, *Aristophanes*. Harcourt, Brace & World, Inc., 1959 and 1962.

Heraklês: Hercules, a very powerful Greek god

Poseidon: Greek god of the sea

hodcarrier: stone carrier

Libya: country in northern Africa

Rails: small marsh birds

Curlews: long-legged birds

Mortar: material containing cement, used in building walls

Herons: long-necked wading birds

hods: trays for carrying stones or mortar

ye: you

trowel: tool for spreading mortar

joists: beams used to support a floor or ceiling

portals: gates or other entrances

Atlantis, The Legend of a Lost City

retold by Christina Balit

For centuries writers have been fascinated by the legend of the lost city of Atlantis. Among those who have written about it are Jules Verne, the famous science fiction writer. The Greek philosopher and writer, Plato, is considered the source for the story. According to Greek legend, the city lies to the west of the Straits of Gibraltar in the Atlantic Ocean. After a violent earthquake, the island was swallowed up by the sea. However, its people are believed to have migrated to other countries, including America. Still others believe that Atlantis was in the West Indies, or was a part of Britain. The most widely accepted theory, however, is found in Egyptian records, which describe a volcanic eruption on the island of Thera. The volcano partially destroyed the island, as well as nearby Crete, which never recovered from the catastrophe. Was Atlantis a fantastic legend, intended as a warning against the dangers of power and ambition? Or, was the story designed to create a permanent record of a natural disaster for future generations? You can decide for yourself as you read this selection.

First there was Chaos. From Chaos sprang Earth and Heaven. From them came the race of Titans; two of them, Cronus and Rheas, seized power and ruled over all. Their son Zeus overthrew them. Then he and his brothers divided up the world: to Zeus went the heavens, to Hades, the **realms** *of the dead, while the seas and oceans went to mighty Poseidon, who promised to guard the waters with care.*

realms: kingdoms or areas

Floating on one of Poseidon's emerald seas was a small rocky island. Few visited its shores and no one bothered to give it a name. But the sun rose warmly over it each morning and set sleepily behind it every night.

In the center of the island there stood a mountain, and at the foot of the mountain lived a man called Evenor and his wife, Leucippe. They lived happily together, working hard to tend the **barren** land, and brought up their daughter Cleito to honor all creatures.

barren: producing little or no vegetation

Poseidon grew curious. How could they be so content with so little? He took on human form and crouched unseen behind a rock to find out.

Each morning at daybreak, he watched Cleito walk over the pebbled ground, barefoot and smiling, to fill her water pot at the stream.

Seeing Cleito in all her beauty, Poseidon's heart grew tender, and one day he stepped out from behind the rock to talk to her. Day after day he came and slowly she began to return his love. Finally she agreed to become his bride. Her parents, unaware of Poseidon's divinity, blessed the union, and a simple wedding followed.

But a god cannot stay hidden. After the wedding, all the spirits of the sea rose to the surface to sing, and Poseidon assumed his divine form once more. He vowed to rebuild the island and make it fit for a king and his queen.

Poseidon used powers beyond human imagining to transform the isle into a paradise.

First, he arranged alternate circles of land and sea—three of land and three of water—to enclose the mountain. Within each circle of land a forest sprang up. Trees bloomed and grew heavy with fruits, and creatures multiplied.

Next, he made a network of canals, fed by waterfalls. Soon the island was yielding two crops each year—one watered by winter rains, the other irrigated by Poseidon's canals. The rich earth was carpeted with herbs and vegetables, and thick with healing roots; from its depths men dug out priceless yellow mountain copper. All things flourished on the sacred island.

Then, under Poseidon's guidance, the inhabitants built a palace fit for a god, with towers, gates, and **parapets** trimmed with gleaming brass and tin. In the center they set up a holy temple dedicated to Poseidon and Cleito, with **pinnacles** of silver surrounded by a wall of gold.

They built thermal baths and **aqueducts,** fountains and gardens—and even a huge racecourse.

It was a happy time for Poseidon and Cleito, and over the years Cleito gave birth to five pairs of twin sons. Their firstborn son they named Atlas. In the summer of his twentieth year he was crowned high king, and they named the island Atlantis in his honor.

Then Poseidon divided the island into ten parts, and gave his sons one-tenth each.

To ensure peace in his new island city, Poseidon set down laws in stone on a pillar of the temple. Chief among them was the commandment that no person should take up arms against another—with a terrible curse on anyone who disobeyed. Every five years, Atlas and the nine princes gathered by night beside the pillar to judge their people according to Poseidon's laws. The people of Atlantis became wise, gentle, and great-spirited. They were sober and kind, as the creator had always wanted them to be. Above all, they lived in peace.

So Atlantis prospered. Its splendid docks were thronged with ships and merchandise, and behind them, a towering lighthouse

parapets: low walls or railings that protect the edge of a platform or roof

pinnacles: lofty peaks

aqueducts: a structure carrying a large quantity of flowing water

lit the way for incoming boats bringing cargoes from other lands. The harbors hummed with trade. Bridges and an underground canal were built to connect the three circles of land around the mountain, as the people grew even richer.

Poseidon, watching from the waves, was content, and went away to his home at the bottom of the sea.

Many years passed, and Poseidon lay sleeping at the bottom of the ocean. The people of Atlantis began to change. Slowly, very slowly, the godlike part of their souls faded and their mortal, human natures took over. They started to argue. Gradually they lost the gift of goodness and became infected with ambition and power. Greed filled the citizens' hearts. The streets of Atlantis, once safe, became dangerous, as people began to steal, cheat, and lie.

One day Zeus, god of gods, who ruled according to the law of the Creator, looked down from the heavens above. He saw the city walls crumbling with neglect, the empty temple, and, worst of all, people fighting one another. He roared out his anger.

The sound of his fury woke Poseidon. Rising to the surface of the waves, the sea-god looked out over his once-perfect kingdom—and wept.

Now he had no choice: he must carry out his terrible curse.

Raising his **trident,** he stirred the seas into a wave that rose so high, it lashed the heavens. The wave vibrated with a roar that could be heard two thousand miles away, and the earth trembled in terror. Gathering its full force, the wave crashed upon the land, while burning rain and ashes blistered down from above.

trident: a 3-pronged spear seen as an attribute of a sea god

In a single day and night, Atlantis was swallowed up by the sea.

Then there was silence. The city sank slowly to its new resting place on the ocean floor.

The people of Atlantis did not die. They continued to exist beneath the waves, but they never spoke or quarreled or fought again. As year followed year they paid a terrible penance, learning to live without gold or possessions in the cold depths. In time, they became little more than creatures of the water.

To this day, Atlantis has never been found. Some people believe that it is still there, under the sea, waiting to be discovered. . . .

This famous legend continues to affect our lives today. The Atlantic Ocean is named after Cleitus' son, Atlas. Atlantis is also the name of a United States space shuttle.

Source: Christina Balit, *Atlantis, The Legend of a Lost City*. New York: Henry Holt and Company, 1999.

THE AENEID

by Virgil, 19 B.C.

The Roman empire left many great monuments, such as the Colosseum, giant aqueducts, and stone roads. But one of Rome's greatest monuments is not a building at all. It is an exciting epic called the Aeneid (ih NEE ihd). This epic, written by the poet Virgil around 19 B.C., is a grand adventure story about the history of Rome. The Aeneid is based on a mythical Trojan character called Aeneas who is half-god and half-man. After the Trojan War, which Homer described in The Iliad on pages 30–32, Aeneas sees a star in the sky and begins a long journey at sea, in hopes of founding a new kingdom. In the excerpt below, Aeneas arrives in Sicily, an island located in the Mediterranean Sea in southern Italy. What do the sporting events that Aeneas orders upon his arrival reveal about some of the values held by people in ancient Rome?

So they shifted their course, and let their ships run before the wind, and came in a very short time to the island of Sicily. Now Acestes, the king of the country, was the son of a Trojan woman. He had before entertained Aeneas and his people very kindly, and now, when he saw their ships coming toward the land, for he happened to be standing on the top of a hill, he was very glad, and he **made haste** to meet them. He came to the shore, having a lion's skin about his shoulders, and carrying a spear in his hand. He greeted them with many words of kindness, and sent a supply of food and drink to the ships.

made haste: hurried

The next day, early in the morning, Aeneas called all the Trojans to an assembly, and said to them: "My friends, it is a full year since we buried my dear father in this land of Sicily; yes, if I remember right, this is the very day. Let us keep it holy therefore. . . . And if the ninth day from this be fair, then we will have great games in honor of my dear father. There shall be a contest of ships, and running in a race, and games of throwing the **javelin**, and of shooting with the bow, and of boxing. . . ."

javelin: spear

And now the ninth day came, and the weather was fine. There came great crowds of people to see the games. . . . Many came to see the Trojans, and many for the sake of the games, desiring to win the prizes if they might. First the prizes were put **in the midst** for all to see. There were crowns of palm, and swords, and spears, and purple garments, and **talents** of gold and silver. . . .

in the midst: in plain view

talents: coins

For [the foot race] there came many, both Trojans and men of Sicily. . . . Aeneas said: "I will give gifts to all who run; none shall go away empty. To the first three I will give crowns of olive. The first also shall have a horse with its **trappings**; the second a **quiver** full of arrows, and a belt with which to fasten it; the third must be content with a Greek helmet."

trappings: saddle and harness

quiver: case for holding arrows

Then all the men stood in a line, and when the signal was given they started. For a short time they were all close together. Then Nisus outran the rest. Next to him came Salius, but there was a long space between them; and next to Salius was Euryalus. The fourth was one of the king's **courtiers**, Helymus by name, and close behind him the Trojan Diores. When they had nearly come to the end of the course, by bad luck Nisus slipped in the blood of an ox which had been **slain** in the place, and fell. But as he lay on the ground he did not forget his friend Euryalus, for he lifted himself from the ground just as Salius came running in, and tripped him up. So Euryalus had the first place, Helymus was second, and Diores third. But Salius loudly complained that he had been cheated. "I had won the first prize," he cried, "had not this Nisus tripped me up." But the people favored Euryalus, for he was a **comely lad**; Diores also was on the same side, for otherwise he had not won the third prize. "Then," said Aeneas, "I will not change the order; let them take the prizes as they come—Euryalus the first, Helymus the second, and Diores the third. Nevertheless I will have pity on the man who suffered not from his own fault." And he gave to Salius a lion's skin, of which the **mane** and the claws were covered with gold. . . .

courtiers: attendants

slain: killed

comely lad: handsome boy

mane: long hair on the neck

Next to this came the trial of shooting with the bow. Aeneas set up the mast of a ship, and to the top of the mast he tied a dove by a cord. This was the mark at which all were to shoot. The first hit the mast, and shook it, and all could see how the bird fluttered his wings. Then the second shot. He did not touch the bird, but he cut the string by which it was fastened to the mast, and the bird flew away. Then the third, a man of Lycia, aimed at the bird itself, and struck it as it flew, and the dove fell dead to the earth with the arrow through it. Last of all King Acestes shot his arrow. And he, having nothing at which to aim, shot it high into the air, to show how strong a bow he had and how he could draw it. Then there happened a strange thing to see. The arrow, as it went higher and higher in the air, was seen to catch fire, and leave a line of flame behind it, till it was burned up. When Aeneas saw this, he said to himself: "This is a sign of good to come," for he thought how the fire had burned on the head of his son Ascanius, and how a star had shot through the air when he was about to fly from Troy. And as this had been a sign of good at the beginning of his wanderings, so was this a sign of good at the end.

After many more adventures, Aeneas helps to unite the people of Italy and Troy. This union, according to the Aeneid, *gave birth to the civilization of Rome. Many people consider the* Aeneid *to be the greatest work of Roman literature.*

Source: Alfred J. Church, *The Aeneid for Boys and Girls.* New York: The Macmillan Company, 1962.

The Eruption of Mount Vesuvius

by Pliny the Younger, A.D. 79

In A.D. 79 Mount Vesuvius, located about seven miles from Naples, Italy, erupted, burying the smaller cities of Pompeii (pahm PAY) and Herculaneum under many feet of mud and volcanic ash. In Pompeii alone, about 2,000 people were killed. A writer named Pliny (PLIHN ee) the Younger (about A.D. 61–113) survived the eruption and wrote letters to the historian Tacitus (TA sih tus) telling about it. As you read this excerpt from one of Pliny's letters, think about the factors that made escape difficult. How are we better prepared to cope with natural disasters today?

For several days before the eruption there had been earth **tremors**, which had not caused much alarm, since they often happen in the Naples area. But that night they were so strong that they not **merely** shook but overturned everything. My mother came running to my bedroom just as I was going to go to awaken her....

tremors: shaking

merely: only

It was now six o'clock in the morning, the daylight still faint and doubtful. The buildings around us were ready to collapse, and so the narrow space where we were was very dangerous. We therefore decided that we must get out of the town. We were followed by a panic-stricken mob of poor people, who pushed us forward by pressing behind us.... A black and horrible cloud belching streamers of fiery snakelike **vapors** split apart every so often to reveal great flaming forms, like lightning but much larger....

vapors: gases

Soon the cloud began to descend upon the earth and cover the sea.... My mother began to beg me to escape as best I could. She said that a young man could do it, while she, slowed by age and weight, would die happily if only she knew that she had not caused my death by her delaying me. I replied that I would not be saved without her and, taking her by the hand, urged her forward. Ashes now fell upon us, thick darkness came rolling over the land like a flood. "Let us leave the road," I said, "while we can still see, so as not to be knocked down and trampled to death in the dark by the crowd behind us."... You could hear the screams of women, the cries of children, the shouts of men.... Many raised their hands to **appeal** to the gods, but more believed that the gods, too, had **perished**, and that the end of the world had come....

appeal: make an earnest request

perished: died

Pliny and his mother were among the lucky ones who escaped. Mount Vesuvius is still an active volcano, last erupting in 1944. Scientists record the temperature at the mouth of Mount Vesuvius every day, since rising temperatures often give warning of an upcoming eruption. Modern archeologists are gradually uncovering Pompeii and Herculaneum. Large portions of the cities are still intact and give us a clear idea of everyday life there.

Source: Hanscom, Hellerman and Posner, eds., *Voices of the Past: Readings in Ancient History.* The Macmillan Company, 1967.

A Craftsman in Bethlehem

by Avram Hissan, 1981

Almost 2,000 years ago a Jewish woman named Mary gave birth to a son in Bethlehem, a town that still exists in Israel today. Mary's son was named Jesus. According to the New Testament of the Bible, Jesus grew up in the town of Nazareth and practiced the religion of Judaism. When he was about 30 years old, Jesus started preaching. As he traveled from village to village, he stressed that love for God required showing love for other people. Jesus won many followers, who called him the Messiah, a term for a special leader sent by God to guide the Jewish people and set up God's rule on Earth. These followers of Jesus began a new religion called Christianity. Avram Hissan is a Christian who lives in Bethlehem. In the excerpt below, Hissan expresses his love for his town and his job. How does Christianity shape his life?

This is a magic city. It's a quiet and friendly town—not so quiet at Christmas, Easter and festivals, when thousands of pilgrims from all over the world pour into our city. Its link with the Jewish people began nearly 4,000 years ago when Jacob, passing through the town, lost his young wife Rachel in childbirth. Bethlehem today has a population of 32,000—mainly Christian Arabs with professions. Many of them are gold smiths, skilled in carving. Every visitor is attracted to the Church of the Nativity, traditionally the birthplace of Jesus, where Mary gave birth and laid the child in the manger because there was no room for him in the inn. The Church of the Nativity is one of the holiest shrines **in Christendom**.

For many generations now we've sold articles carved in olive wood and also goods made of mother-of-pearl. They are the most sought-after goods in Bethlehem, extremely popular with the tourists. The olive-wood industry is famous here. We have our own factory beneath our store where we make all kinds of figures and nativity sets. The majority of the olive-wood goods sold in the store are made on the premises.

in Christendom:
among Christian
worshipers

We call olive wood the holy wood. We carve very large pieces too—large manger sets are bought and taken all over the world, especially at Christmas time.

Thank God, without religion we cannot live. I pray in St. Mary's Church in Bethlehem. Our services are held in the **Aramaic** language in our churches all over the world. This was the language of the Lord Our Saviour, and of our **Prophets**, Abraham, Isaac and Jacob.

I work in the store every day from 8 o'clock [in the morning] until 7 or 8 o'clock in the evening. On Sundays I go to church in the morning and then go to work. I like to take vacations, but only a day at a time. I usually go with my brother George. I like to go in and around Bethlehem, sometimes to King Solomon's Pools. This is one of our main beauty spots; it's fertile and the pool is spring-fed. . . . It was erected some 500 years ago, and is now ringed by a well-grown pine forest. These great open reservoirs form a green and beautiful park, an ideal picnic spot.

I also like to go to Jericho and to the Dead Sea where the climate is much warmer and drier than here. I'm very much a family man and I enjoy staying at home in the evenings with my family; so many friends come in to visit us and, of course, business people, mainly from the United States.

Christians and Moslems live together in Bethlehem. We have very good relations with the Jews; we have lived together now for fourteen years. We are happy and we hope for peace in the future.

Christianity spread rapidly throughout the Roman empire and much of Europe. It also spread into Africa and Asia. Europeans later introduced Christianity to other parts of the world. Today nearly 2 billion people—or almost one in three people int he world—are Christians. To learn about another important religion that emerged in western Asia, read the selection on pages 45–46.

Aramaic: ancient language used widely in the Middle East from 600 B.C. to A.D. 800

prophets: persons who deliver messages believed to be from God

Source: Gemma Levine, *We Live in Israel.* New York: The Bookwright Press, 1983.

FROM
MOUSE TO BAT

Maya Fable Retold by Victor Montejo, 1991

Between A.D. 250 and A.D. 900, the ancient Maya had a rich civilization in what are today the countries of Mexico, Guatemala, Honduras, and El Salvador. They left many written records of their civilization in the form of books and temples carved with glyphs and other pictures. They also left oral records such as fables, stories, and tales that have been passed down from one generation to the next. This practice of using fables to teach a lesson has continued to the present day. Victor Montejo (mahn TAY hoh), a Maya born in 1952, recently collected some of the fables and stories that he heard while growing up in Guatemala. As you read this Maya fable, try to determine the moral of the story.

When the Creator and Shaper made all the animals, each **species** was eager to know where they would live, and he assigned their **habitats** to them.

The happiest were the birds who flew singing to the trees to build their nests. Only *Tx'ow* [tshoh], the mouse, didn't move. He stood there open-mouthed **contemplating** the marvelous flight of the birds.

"Go on," the Creator told him. "Go eat the kernels of corn, seeds, and all the forgotten pieces of food."

But *Tx'ow* wouldn't move. His body shook with resentment.

The Creator, very angry, picked him up by the tail and threw him in the bush. *Tx'ow* still could not say a word. He only stared at the flight of the singing birds with his eyes popping out. Then he looked at himself and became very sad. He could make little jumps, but fly? No, he could never achieve that.

species: category of animals
habitats: places to live

contemplating: thinking about

43

Now is the time to act, he said to himself. He decided to call together all the members of his species. There weren't many in those times. Well, he thought, they must be as discontented as I am.

Tx'ow easily convinced his brothers and sisters that they deserved more. One afternoon the **delegation** of mice came before the god, as he rested from the work of creation.

delegation: group

"What do you want? Speak up," he ordered them.

The delegation tried to speak but it could not. All they could say was, *witz'itz'i, witz'itz'i* [weets eets EE].

The wise god understood what they had come for and he said to them, "You want to fly like the birds?"

The delegation broke out in a big racket of *witz'itz'i, witz'itz'i* nodding their heads yes.

"Very good," the Creator said, "Tomorrow you should appear at *tx'eqwob'al* [tshay kwoh BAHL], the place for jumping, and I will give you your opportunity."

The mice went away satisfied, believing that a favorable **resolution** was at hand. To celebrate, there was a great rejoicing among the [tree] roots that night.

resolution: outcome

When the sun came up, the Creator was waiting at the place he had chosen to meet the unhappy mice. "Ready for the test?" he asked. "Those who can jump over this **ravine** will instantly receive wings and go flying away. And those who do not succeed will remain as they are."

ravine: steep valley

The discontented mice filed up one by one and launched out on the grand adventure. Those whose efforts carried them to the other side received wings and went flying off to the caverns, looking still like mice except for their wings. Those who did not succeed resigned themselves to their fate.

When the great test was over, the Creator warned them, "I don't want you returning to bother me anymore. You who are mice will continue eating grain and seeds. If you want, you can climb the trees and make your nests there. On the other hand those who now have wings will from now on be called *Sotz'* [sohtz], the bats. For them day will be night. They will feed on mosquitoes and blood, and sleep hanging upside down from the walls of *nhach'en* [nah CHAYN], the caverns, today and forever."

So it was that *Tx'ow,* the mouse, learned to accept himself and understood that his relatives, the bats, had not found happiness in their new condition either. They lost their tails and their toes grew long in order to cling to the rocks.

Today about 4 million Maya live in Mexico and the countries of Central America. The oral tradition—the passing down of stories, beliefs, and history—remains a central part of Maya culture.

Source: Victor Montejo, *The Bird Who Cleans the World and Other Mayan Fables.* Willimantic, CT: Curbstone Press, 1991.

Pilgrimage to Mecca

by Samaan bin Jabir Al Nasaib, 1987

During the seventh century a major religion called Islam emerged in the Middle East. According to Islamic faith, around A.D. 610 an Arab merchant named Muhammad heard a voice tell him that there is only one God—for which the Arabic word is Allah—and that he, Muhammad, was Allah's messenger. Followers of Muhammad's teachings became known as Muslims, or "followers of Islam." After Muhammad's death these teachings were gathered into a book called the Quran (Kaw RAN). The Quran is believed by Muslims to be the teachings of God. The Quran teaches that Muhammad is the last in the line of prophets, or people who deliver a message believed to be from God. Muslims believe that earlier prophets were Abraham, Moses, and Jesus. One of the duties that all Muslims try to fulfill at least once in their lives is to make a journey to the city of Mecca, the birthplace of Muhammad. What is this journey like? In the following selection from an oral history, a Muslim from Saudi Arabia named Samaan bin Jabir Al Nasaib describes his recent pilgrimage to Mecca. What are some of the rituals that Jabir Al Nasaib performs during his pilgrimage? How do these rituals relate to his religious beliefs?

My family traces its **descent** from the oldest of the tribes of this part of the world. Some say that we can trace our heritage back to Adam. Whether or not this is so, we have been landowners and **sheikhs** in the **Wadi Najran** for as long as anybody can remember. We grow corn, wheat and citrus fruit here.

I suppose the high spot of my life was performing the Hajj [hahj] in the company of my son Maana. The Hajj is the name we give to the pilgrimage that Muslims make to Mecca, to the Holy Kaaba [KAH buh], Abraham's "House of God." This pilgrimage is one of the "five pillars of Islam," the other four being the belief in one God, prayer five times a day, the giving of **alms** and fasting during the holy month of Ramadan. What a proud and spiritually rewarding moment it was for me to make my seven rounds of the Kaaba with my son beside me!

The Hajj requires great physical stamina as well as religious **zeal**. The Hajjis, as pilgrims are called, must all wear a special garment consisting of two white lengths of cotton, without seams, emphasizing the equality of all men in the sight of God. We put the garment on at the start of our journey, after ritual washing and prayer.

On arrival in Mecca, after further washing and prayer, the pilgrims go directly to the Kaaba and circle it seven times in an anti-clockwise

descent: origins

sheikhs: Arab leaders

Wadi Najran: region in southwest Saudi Arabia

alms: aid to the poor

zeal: enthusiasm

45

direction. On passing the Black Stone, they should try either to kiss it or at least touch it. This stone is a meteorite and is traditionally held to be a link between the Prophet **Mohammed**, Abraham and Adam.

Mohammed: Muhammad

After the duties of the Kaaba, pilgrims are required to run between two hills, Al Safa and Al Marwah, which both have links with Abraham's wife, Hagar. While doing this they are praying all the while. Pilgrims may then drink from the spring of Zam Zam, which is referred to in the Old Testament [of the Bible]. Male pilgrims then have their heads shaved, or more commonly today, their hair cut.

Now follows a visit to Mount Arafat, where Mohammed gave his farewell sermon. A whole afternoon is spent in the open air, on the Plain of Arafat, standing bareheaded, glorifying God and reading the **Koran**.

Koran: Quran

Crowds of pilgrims spend the night under the stars at Musdalifah, and each collects seventy small pebbles. Then they make their way to Mina, the end of the journey, where there are three stone pillars. Seven of the pebbles are then cast at the pillars, an act symbolic of mankind casting out the evil from within. Then animals are sacrificed and the meat given to the poor. Before returning home, the pilgrims throw the remaining pebbles at the pillars.

The pilgrimage ends after a final symbolic cutting of hair. Some pilgrims take this opportunity of going on to Medina, where they can visit the Tomb of Mohammed, and the Prophet's **Mosque**.

mosque: Islamic house of worship

Back on my farm in the Wadi Najran, I often remember those privileged days I spent in Mecca.

Today over 1 billion people—or about one in six people in the world—are Muslims. Judaism, Christianity, and Islam all emerged in western Asia. Thousands of miles to the east, two other major religions also developed long ago. To learn more about these other two religions, read the documents on pages 22–23 and 24–25.

Source: Abdul Latif Al Hoad, *We Live in Saudi Arabia*. New York: The Bookwright Press, 1987.

An Islamic Hospital

by Abdul-Wáhid al-Marrakhshí, about 1200

Between the late 700s and the 1200s, Islamic culture became very powerful and influential. The Muslim caliphate, centered in Baghdad, ruled many lands in parts of western Asia, northern Africa, and southern Europe. The people of the Islamic civilization were known for outstanding achievements in many areas including medical care. Ibn Sina (IHB un SEE nuh) (980–1037), a Muslim doctor, wrote medical textbooks with ideas that were far ahead of their time. His contributions to medical knowledge are still recognized as valuable. The following selection by Abdul-Wáhid al-Marrakhshí (ab dul WAY ihd al ma rak SHEE) describes one of the most famous Islamic hospitals, at Marrakesh, Morocco, in North Africa. As you read, consider how this hospital might differ from a modern hospital.

Here was constructed a hospital, which I think is unequalled in the world. First there was selected a large open space in the most level part of the town. Orders were given to architects to construct a hospital as well as possible. So the workmen **embellished** it with a beauty of sculpture and ornamentation even beyond what was demanded of them. All sorts of suitable trees and fruit trees were planted there. Water there was **in abundance**, flowing through all the rooms. . . .

embellished: decorated

in abundance: plentiful

A daily allowance of thirty **dinars** was assigned for the daily ration of food, exclusive of the drugs and chemicals which were on hand for the preparation of **draughts, unguents, and collyria**. For the use of the patients there were provided day-dresses and night-dresses, thick for winter, thin for summer.

dinars: gold coins

draughts, unguents, and collyria: medicines

After he was cured, a poor patient received on leaving the hospital a sum of money **sufficient** to keep him for a time. Rich patients received back their money and clothes. In short, the Founder did not **confine** the use of the hospital to the poor or to the rich. **On the contrary**, every stranger who fell ill at Marrakesh was carried there and treated until he either recovered or died. Every Friday the Prince after the mid-day prayer mounted his horse to go and visit the patients and to learn about each of them. He used to ask how they were and how they were being treated. This was his use until the day of his death.

sufficient: enough

confine: restrict

On the contrary: instead

The Islamic government also had "moving hospitals" that took beds and medical supplies by camel to places where patients could not get to a hospital.

Source: Cyril Elgood, *A Medical History of Persia and the Eastern Caliphate.* London: Cambridge University Press Associated, 1951. Reprint 1979.

NEW FORCES IN THE WORLD

*The mind of a painter should be like
a mirror, which always takes the
color of the object it reflects and is
filled by the images of as many
objects as are in front of it . . .
you cannot be a good painter unless
you represent . . . every kind of
form produced by nature.*

Leonardo da Vinci, 1482

"Tortoise, Hare, and the Sweet Potatoes"

retold by Ashley Bryan

Before people kept written records of their culture, they relied on oral story telling to pass on their traditions from one generation to the next. Today these entertaining tales reveal the beliefs and customs of a particular culture to modern readers. Although the purpose of folk tales was to entertain the listeners, these imaginative stories often teach a lesson as well. Animals, who talk and behave like humans, are often characters in these stories. As you read, notice how the animals display human qualities. What does this folk tale say about being greedy and sly?

Listen, brothers and sisters, to this story of how Tortoise outwitted Hare.

Hare was born a trickster. He was always dreaming up new riddles and tricks to try on others. He'd spring an impossible riddle, wait a little, then rattle off the answer. Riddles and tricks, Hare never tired of either.

Tortoise on the other hand was much too busy keeping her little pond clean to worry about tricking anyone. Animals came from field and forest, far and near, to drink in the pond where she lived.

Tortoise believed in the proverb, "Give the passing traveler water and you will drink news yourself." So, although she rarely left her pool, her visitors kept her well informed. She knew more than most and was seldom fooled.

It happened one season then that the news Tortoise heard again and again was disgracefully bad. Someone was stealing food from all the fields around. Now most creatures were willing to give when another was hungry. But stealing was taboo.

Everyone asked, "Who would do what's taboo?" And no one knew. But Tortoise had a few well-founded ideas.

One day Hare came by Tortoise's pond. He drank his fill, then was ready for mischief. "Aha! Now to muddy the pond and have a little fun," he thought. He had never cared for the **proverb,** "Do not fill up the well with mud after having drunk. Where would you drink tomorrow?"

Tortoise was on her guard, however, and all Hare could do was sit beside her and ask riddles. Tortoise answered every one.

"I know one you can't answer," said Hare. "Tell me the thing that you can beat without leaving a scar."

"I live by it and I drink it," said Tortoise. "Water."

proverb: a short saying that expresses something believed to be true

50

So Hare gave up trying to catch Tortoise with riddles. But he was not through.

After a while he said, "Now old tortoise, let's go and till a field together."

"Me! Till the land? I can just manage to scratch out my little garden patch. How could I hoe a whole field with my short legs?"

"Short legs? Your legs are beautiful. Just the right length for hoeing."

"Do say! But how could I hold a hoe?"

"No problem at all. I'll tie you to it. I'd love to do that for you."

There was truth in that statement, Tortoise decided. Hare knew how to trick people, all right. But she wasn't taken in. She said aloud, "I don't think I'll try, thanks."

So they sat in silence. And after a while Hare said, "I'm hungry, Sis. Aren't you?"

"A little, but I don't have a leaf left in my garden."

"Well, poor thing. Let me help you. I came upon a wide field of good things on my way here. Come on! Let's help ourselves to some of Wild Boar's sweet potatoes."

"Ooo,ooo! What are you saying? You know better than that Mr. Hare. No **pilfering!**"

pilfering: stealing in small quantities

So they sat on in silence, Hare not willing to give up.

"Where did you say that field of sweet potatoes was?" she asked.

"It's not far, just past the bush."

"Well now," said Tortoise, seeming to overcome her **scruples,** "I guess Wild Boar won't miss a few."

scruples: hesitation on grounds of conscience

Off they went together. And when they came to Wild Boar's field it was no job at all to root out the sweet potatoes. Soon Hare's sack was filled.

Hare with a great show of strength steadied the bag on Tortoise's back, and they headed for the bush to cook the potatoes. When they found a good quiet spot, they gathered dry grass and made a crackling fire in which the sweet potatoes were soon roasted.

"Mmm-yum," said Tortoise, her mouth full of sweet potato.

"Stop munching and mumbling!" said Hare. "What if we're caught?"

'Mmm-um-yum," said Tortoise, reaching for another sweet potato.

"Wow-wow," said Hare, "do you want to be beaten and bitten by Wild Boar? Put down that potato! We've got to scout around first and make sure that Boar's not after us."

Tortoise, who had a good notion of what was afoot and was ready, waddled a few reluctant steps; Hare bounded out of sight. As soon as he was gone, Tortoise turned back, took another sweet potato, and crawled into the empty sack.

"Mmm-yum," she said. She was about to crawl out for another when suddenly a rain of roasted sweet potatoes fell around her. Hare was back, very quietly, very quickly.

"Good," said Tortoise, biting into another sweet potato, "saves me the trouble."

Old trickster Hare filled his sack in a hurry.

"Mistress Tortoise," he shouted then. "Get going! Take off! Run for your life! Wild Boar and his big fat wife are coming."

He threw the bag over his back. "Save yourself! Fly!" he cried, but inside he thought: "Best trick in ages. Now to put some miles between me and Slowpoke."

Tortoise made herself comfortable in the sack. She ate one sweet potato after another. "Too bad Hare is missing the feast," she thought. "But maybe he prefers running to eating."

Hare ran as fast and as far as he could. By the time he stopped to rest, Tortoise had eaten all the finest and fattest sweet potatoes. In fact, there was only one very small sweet potato left.

"Aha good," said Hare as he put his hand into the sack. "Too bad Tortoise is miles away."

"Sweet potatoes," Hare sang, "sweet, sw-eeeet potatoes!" Tortoise put the last sweet potato into Hare's outstretched hand.

When Hare saw the size of it, he cried, "Ha! What a miserable one this is. I didn't run my head off for that!" And he flung it into the bushes. Hare put his hand back into the sack. This time he felt a big one, a nice firm juicy one. "Oho!" he chortled. "Here's a beauty. What a prize!"

Imagine Hare's surprise when he saw what he had in his hand.

"Mistress Tortoise!" he cried as he dropped her to the ground.

Hare shook out the sack. Tears of unbelief welled up in his eyes when he saw it was empty. "My potatoes, the sweet ones I rooted up…oh no, oh no! You didn't eat mine, too? Sister Tortoise, how could you be so unfair?"

But Mistress Tortoise didn't stand around for the lecture. She took to her toes and **scuttled** away to her pond as fast as she could go.

> **scuttled:** a quick shuffling pace

Hungry Hare lay on the ground and screeched, "Woe, woe, that wily Mistress Tortoise ate all my sweet potatoes. Wa, Waa. How awful of her. When I think I carried her all the while, I could cry!"

And that's just what he did.

In this folktale, Hare is described as a "trickster," who tries to outsmart his opponent, Tortoise. In North American Indian stories from California and the Southwest, the trickster was a coyote. In folktales from parts of Africa, the trickster was the hare.

Source: Ashley Bryan, *Ashley Bryan's African Tales, UH-HUH.* New York: Atheneum Books for Young Readers, 1998.

Aïda

retold by Leontyne Price

For more than a hundred years the story of Aïda, the Ethiopian princess, who is enslaved in Egypt, has thrilled audiences. It is the subject of a famous opera by the Italian composer, Giuseppe Verdi. Leontyne Price, who retells the story in this selection, has a special connection to Aïda. Ms. Price is one of the greatest American opera singers of the 20th century. She has performed the title role in Aïda many times in her career, beginning in San Francisco in 1957. In talking about the importance of the character, she has said: "Aïda has given me great inspiration onstage and off. Her deep devotion and love for her country and for her people—her nobility, strength, and courage—are all qualities I aspire to as a human being. I will never forget her." As you read this excerpt from the story, think about the heroic qualities that Aïda possesses. How does her tremendous love for her country and her people affect her life?

Long ago, in the faraway land of Ethiopia, there lived a princess named Aïda. She was fair as the sunrise and gentle as starlight touching a flower. Her father, the great Amonasro, loved her dearly.

It was a time of terrible fear and danger in Ethiopia, for the kingdom was at war with its neighbor, Egypt. Both countries raided each other's lands, killing or enslaving their enemies.

For the safety of his people, King Amonasro set strict boundaries at the borders of his country, and no Ethiopian was allowed beyond them.

The Princess Aïda was young and, locked within the palace, she grew restless. So, one morning, Aïda and her trusted friends disobeyed the King's command. They disguised themselves and slipped away from the palace guards.

It was a glorious day of freedom, out in the gentle breezes and lush green fields of their beautiful country. But Aïda wandered farther than she should have. Off on her own, enjoying the warm sun and fresh country air, she did not hear her friends in the distance when they shouted, "Aïda! Beware! Come back!"

Once again, Egyptian soldiers had invaded Ethiopia, crossing the south edge of the River Nile. Now they marched toward Aïda.

When she finally did hear her friends' warning, it was too late. Soldiers seized her. Bound with ropes and chains, Aïda, the Royal Princess of Ethiopia, was carried off to Egypt as a slave.

53

Aïda had learned her royal lessons well. She revealed to no one that she was the daughter of King Amonasro of Ethiopia. But her beauty and noble bearing attracted great attention. So sparkling and unusual was she that the all-powerful Pharaoh, the ruler of Egypt, chose her from among thousands of captured slaves to be his gift—a personal handmaiden—to his only daughter, the Princess Amneris.

It was easy for Aïda to perform the duties of a servant, for she remembered what her own handmaidens had done. The Egyptian Princess Amneris was fascinated, for Aïda was different from any slave she had ever seen. She wanted her new handmaiden to be her closest companion. Even with the special privileges granted to one so close to the Royal Princess, Aïda felt nothing but despair. All her life she had been the beloved daughter of Ethiopia's King, and now she was a slave to her father's enemy. She knew there was no hope of ever seeing Ethiopia again.

There was one source of light in her life, however. For Radames, the handsome young captain of the Egyptian Army, had fallen in love with the gentle, beautiful slave the moment he saw her. She, too, had fallen for Radames, despite his position as an enemy of her homeland.

"I will lead the Egyptian Army to victory," he told her, "and when I return, our countries will be united, and you will become my bride and reign as the Queen of your people. It will not be long, I promise."

The day finally came when the Pharaoh was to hold court and announce the new leader of the war against Ethiopia.

Amid the majestic columns of a great hall in the palace, Egypt's high Priest, Ramfis confided to Radames: "There are rumors that the Ethiopians plan to attack. Prepare yourself, for the Goddess Isis has chosen, and the great honor of leadership may be bestowed upon you."

All his life, Radames had dreamed of this day. If he became the new leader, he could return triumphant to free Aïda and marry her. "Ah, heavenly Aïda," he thought. "I could finally enthrone you in your native land."

Radames was deep in thought when Princess Amneris stepped from the shadows. She, too, was in love with the handsome leader, but she suspected he loved another.

Aïda suddenly appeared.

Oh, how Radames's eyes filled with passion! And when Amneris saw the look that passed between them, she was seized with suspicion and jealousy. Could Radames prefer a *slave* to the Princess of Egypt? It was intolerable! But her fury was interrupted by trumpets heralding the arrival of the Pharoah.

A messenger came forward to give his report.

"Mighty Pharoah, the Ethiopians have attacked. They are led by the fierce warrior King Amonasro, who has invaded Egypt!"

A thunder of anger broke out in court, and upon hearing her father's name, Aïda quietly cried out in fear.

The Pharoah rose, and the crowd grew still.

"Radames will lead our army," he cried. "It is the decree of the Goddess Isis. Death to the Ethiopians! Victory to Egypt!" he shouted. "Return victorious, Radames!" he commanded.

"Return victorious! Return victorious!" the throng shouted, and Aïda, too, was stirred by the cry. In spite of herself, she also began to shout, "Return victorious! Return victorious!" as the court led the soldiers off to battle. Aïda was now left alone.

"Return victorious!" she called after Radames, but as her own voice echoed in the great hall, she suddenly realized she was asking for the death of her father, her mother, her friends, and all those she cherished. Yet how could she pray for the death of the man she loved?

Aïda was shocked. Her heart was torn between Radames and her loyalty to her father and Ethiopia. She fell to her knees and prayed.

"Oh, great gods of my youth!" she cried. "Pity me!"

That night, the halls of the temple rang as the priestesses chanted the sacred **consecration** song. The High Priest, Ramfis, led prayers to Phtha, the creator of life and mightiest Egyptian god, as he gave the great hero the sacred sword of Egypt.

consecration: dedicated to a sacred purpose

"Let the sword of Radames be the strength of our nation! Let his bravery in battle crush the Ethiopians! Protect our land," they prayed, "and make Radames the most magnificent warrior of all."

With Radames gone, time passed slowly for Aïda. But soon the prayers of the priestesses were granted. A special day dawned for Egypt—a day of ceremony and grandeur, of **pomp** and **pageantry.** The Ethiopians had been defeated at last.

pomp and pageantry: splendid display, spectacle

Amneris sat before her mirror. Surrounded by slaves and adorned in her most beautiful gown and jewels, she was pleased with her reflection. Surely today when Radames returned, he would be struck by her radiance. Yet despite her vanity, she secretly burned with jealousy to think that Aïda, a mere handmaiden, might truly be loved by Radames.

So Amneris decided to test her privileged slave. And when gentle Aïda entered the royal chambers, Amneris sobbed, pretending great grief.

"Oh, Aïda, Aïda!" she cried in a shaking voice. "Egypt has lost its finest warrior. Radames has been killed in battle!"

Immediately Aïda wept with the pain of one whose heart has been broken forever. There was no longer any doubt in Amneris's mind.

"It is all a lie!" she shouted. "Radames was not killed. He lives!"

Aïda's tears of sorrow turned to tears of joy.

Overcome with fury, Amneris hurled Aïda to the floor. "How dare you, a lowly slave, love the same man loved by the Princess of Egypt!"

But Aïda, too, was a Princess. She rose proudly. She was about to tell Amneris the truth, but she stopped herself. Instead, with great difficulty she asked to be forgiven.

"Have mercy on me," she begged. "Your power is unquestioned—you have all that a person could want. But what do I have to live for? My love of Radames, and that alone."

Aïda's plea only fueled Amneris's rage. She stormed out of the chamber, leaving Aïda to fear the worst.

Flags flew, and the entire city gathered to see the grand spectacle of the victory parade led by the Pharaoh, the Princess, and the High Priest. Trumpets blared, and dancing girls threw rose petals to form a welcoming carpet before the magnificent chariot of Radames.

"Hail to the conqueror!" they roared. "Hail to Radames!"

The Pharoah proclaimed, "Radames, you are my greatest soldier. As a reward, whatever you wish shall be yours."

When Radames rose, he saw Aïda. Amneris saw the look of love on his face, and she was consumed with jealousy. Yet he dared not asked for Aïda's hand, not at that moment in public court.

"Mighty Pharoah," he said instead, "I ask that you allow me to call forth our prisoners of war."

The Pharaoh granted Radames's request, and the Ethiopians were led into the square in chains. One tall, proud man stood out above the rest. Aïda gasped. It was her father!

The crowd was shocked to see her run and embrace him, but he whispered to her, "Do not betray that I am King."

Amonasro addressed the Pharaoh. "I am Aïda's father, and I have faithfully fought for my sovereign, who died in battle. I am prepared to die for him and my country, but I **beseech** you to have mercy on those who have been defeated."

beseech: to beg for urgently or anxiously

With outstretched arms, Aïda joined the Ethiopians. "Let the prisoners go free," she begged Radames and the Pharaoh.

So moved by her appeal, the Egyptian people joined in, and their cries urged the Pharaoh to allow the captured soldiers to be released.

What do you think will happen to Aïda, Amonasro, and Radames? How will Ethiopia avenge its Egyptian conquerors? At the end of the story, Aïda demonstrates her devotion and bravery. She is truly an unforgettable heroine.

Source: Leontyne Price, *Aïda*. San Diego: Gulliver Books, 1990.

Mansa Musa
by Khephra Burns

In the 1300's the western African empire of Mali controlled much of the world's gold supply. As a result, Mali was extremely wealthy, and the wealthiest person of all was the King or Sultan. His name was Mansa Musa, and it was said of him that: "So abundant was the gold which is found in his country that he is the richest and most notable king in the land." During his reign, the Malian Empire was larger and richer than Egypt. Although historians have researched Mansa Musa's reign and the importance of the Mali Empire, very little is known about his childhood. The author of the book from which this selection is taken, created that part of his story. As you read this adventure, which begins when the future king was only fourteen years old, consider how these events shaped his character. What do you think the young Mansa Musa, also known as Kankan, learned when he was taken from his village? How do you think he felt about the mysterious stranger who saved him?

The two young women of the village brought out milk, sweetmeats, and kola nuts, for the visitor. Kola nuts, especially, were considered a luxury among the desert peoples, who prized them not only for their refreshment, but because the embrace of the "twins"—the two interlocking kernels of the nut—made them a token of friendship.

The stranger loosed his veil, revealing a face so black it was almost blue. He told them his name was Tariq al-Aya and that he was a member of the Tuareg tribe from the north. He told strange tales of the great sea to the west where the world begins and ends and of his travels across the vast desert to the north and east.

It seemed to Kankan that the Tuareg spoke directly to him as he told of a sea of sand whose waving dunes rise and fall as far as the eye can see; where billowing dust hangs on the hot wind, blotting out the horizon during the day; where it can become so cold at night that water turns to diamonds, only to become water again when the sun rises; and where terrible sand storms can eat the flesh off a man's bones and etch the bones to slivers.

He told of the mischievous jinns—genies who cause travelers to see mirages, like green oases full of date palms, flowers, and flowing water where, in reality, there is only more sand. "Jinns can put you to sleep, show you miracles, and even transport you through the air. The desert holds many mysteries," he said. "It is a place where many are lost, but it is also a place where a few truly find themselves.

"And beyond the desert there are worlds where great nations like al-Khemia raise temples to rival the mountains, and wise men go to study and learn. There, too, is Mecca, where all roads converge."

57

Mecca, Kankan knew, was the sacred city of Islam, the Muslim faith. Like many in Kaba Kangaba, Kankan's family had converted to Islam but, at the same time, they had not given up their traditional religious practices or their belief in the ancestors. And no one from the village had ever been to Mecca.

"Beyond the desert," the stranger added, "few take any notice of the Malinke of Mali."

Kankan bristled at this. He wanted to say that Mali would again be great and to tell of Abubakari's dream of carrying its fame to worlds beyond the western sea. But it was not Kankan's place to speak. He was young yet—only fourteen—and it had been less than a year since he was initiated into the company of the adult men of the village. If he were a *simbon*—a master hunter who could communicate with the spirits of the forest and bush—he would speak and everyone would listen. But he had not yet hunted his first lion, and for the present he had to sit quietly and listen while others spoke.

Suddenly the night was shattered by loud cries in an unfamiliar tongue rushing in from the darkness. Men on foot and on horses seemed to be everywhere, filling the village with dust and blood and screams. Slave raiders! Kankan and Abubakari ran for their spears. But before they reached their weapons, someone threw a raffia sack over Kankan and he was swallowed up in darkness. Above the noise of the **melee** he heard his mother and brother calling, "Kankan! Kankan!" But there was nothing he could do. As he was thrown over a horse and carried away, their voices faded along with the sounds of the chaos that filled the village.

melee: a confused struggle

Hours passed. Kankan, angry and ashamed to find himself captured and carried off like a child, saw nothing and heard only the sound of the horses' hooves. He vowed to remain alert and to seize the first opportunity to escape. The horses slowed to a walk, and Kankan listened intently. Perhaps, he thought, the slave raiders would stop to rest and he would have his chance. But they kept moving at this slower pace for many more hours, and eventually Kankan drifted into sleep, exhausted.

As Kankan awakened, he knew that something was different, but first he could not figure out just what it was. He rubbed the sleep from his eyes and found himself looking at a strange landscape. It was not the **millet,** rice, or yam fields of Kaba Kangaba. It was not the pastureland where the herdsmen grazed their cattle. It was not the forest. It was nothing! The world seemed to have disappeared.

millet: a grass cultivated for its grain

Then Kankan remembered the raid on his village. He turned around, and a short distance away he saw a camp of four camel-hair tents. Around them he saw horses, camels, and men—blue men, probably Tuareg, in flowing robes, with turbans and veils that left only their eyes visible. The silver handles of their swords glinted in the harsh sunlight from beneath the layered folds of fabric.

Remembering his plan to escape, Kankan rose to his feet but took only a few steps. He was weak. His legs were wobbly, and as he looked around, he realized that there was no place to run—no tree, no rock to hide him—only mile after mile of shifting sand dunes stretching to the horizon in every direction. Heat rising from the sand set the air **aquiver.** Kankan looked back. The Tuareg nomads were watching him but made no move toward him. It took all of Kankan's strength just to keep standing, so for the present, he sat back down.

aquiver: marked by trembling

One of the blue men gave orders, and a moment later Kankan saw someone approaching who looked familiar. It was Yaya, one of the boys of Kankan's age group who must have been captured also. Yaya brought him water and something to eat. "Kankan, you have returned," said Yaya. "You were asleep for many days, and the raiders decided only this morning to leave you to die in the desert."

Kankan gradually regained his strength and was not left to die. Instead, he remained a captive of the desert band. Together with the others from his village, he was bound to his captors not by rope but by his need for food and water. The caravan moved in the early morning hours before the sun rose, and rested during the day when the sun was high in the sky. Then, in late afternoon, they would set off again and continue for some time into the night, always moving toward the northeast.

After several days they came to an oasis where there were date palms and henna trees, houses that were square or rectangle, unlike the round houses of Kankan's village, and a market where traders bartered glass beads, spices, brocade, slaves, and salt for gold.

As they entered the market, Kankan looked back toward the desert from which they had taken refuge and saw another band of blue men on camelback, their voluminous robes billowing, their faces veiled to protect them from the biting winds and blowing sands. As the men drew closer there appeared to be only three of them, then two, then one. Their number had been a mirage, a trick of the desert.

The lone traveler dismounted and approached the captives. He looked over the group and then stopped in front of Kankan, staring at him with hard eyes. Silver **talismans** to ward off the evil eye encircled his turban and glinted in the afternoon sunlight. He turned and walked away, but returned moments later with one of the slave traders. The lone traveler pointed to Kankan as the men spoke in their strange language. Gold changed hands, and then the slaver grasped Kankan roughly by

talismans: an object held to act as a charm to bring good luck

59

the arm and pulled him up from where he was sitting on the ground.

The nomad mounted his kneeling camel, and the beast lurched to its feet. Looking down at Kankan and pointing to another animal, the veiled blue black stranger said, "Take that camel and come." Kankan took the reins of the beast and led it out of the oasis and into the open desert, following his uncertain fate. Sadness weighed heavily on his heart. *I am not just a captive, but a slave*, he thought. *And I may never see my village again.*

Late that night they made a camp. When Kankan had traveled with the slave raiders, he and other captives slept in the open. He never saw the inside of the Tuaregs' tents. But this nomad was different. "Come," he said. Cautiously, warily, Kankan entered the camel-hair tent. Inside he found surprising comforts. The ceilings and walls of the tent were hung with silk tapestries, and rich rugs carpeted the floors. Light flickered from three oil wicks, and incense filled the air.

Kankan also spied a curved knife. While the desert wanderer was occupied with laying out food of some sort, he turned his back to Kankan. Kankan picked up the knife and removed it from his sheath. If he moved quickly, he could take the man by surprise. His whole body trembled with readiness, yet something held him back.

With his back still to Kankan, the wanderer poured tea, and said casually, "It is a difficult thing when one is young . . . knowing when to act and when to watch and wait."

Kankan froze where he stood, unable to move a muscle. Had the man seen him pick up the knife? And if so, why had he not turned to defend himself?

"The blood one spills with fearful stabs at phantoms in the dark," said the nomad, "may turn out to be the water from one's own waterskin when the harsh light of day returns to the desert."

The Tuareg's words were a warning, and Kankan knew he was right; even with camels and water, Kankan would never survive alone in this alien world. Kankan slipped the blade back into its sheath and laid it down.

A moment later the nomad turned toward him with an offering of food: pounded millet served with milk and honey in a half **calabash,** dried meat, tea, and kola nuts. Looking now into Kankan's eyes, the Tuareg counseled, "In the desert, death is always near at hand, as familiar as a frequent guest for whom one has developed deep respect. It is even at times a friend." He paused and then added, "There is no greater freedom than freedom from the fear of death."

There was something familiar about this man, something that lay just beyond Kankan's recognition.

calabash: a gourd

"Sit and eat," the man commanded. The food looked good and Kankan was very hungry, so for the present, he put aside his vague suspicions and ate.

When Kankan looked up again, he saw the Tuareg had loosed his veiled, and to Kankan's amazement, he was the same man who had visited Kaba Kangaba the night the slave raiders came—Tariq al-Aya.

"You!" Kankan jumped to his feet. "My village offered you hospitality."

"And so I offer you the same now," replied Tariq, his voice calm.

"You betrayed us to the slave raiders!" Kankan said.

"I am not one of them," the nomad told him. His words had the ring of truth, but Kankan was reluctant to believe him.

"But you bought me to be your slave," Kankan said accusingly.

"You are your own slave," Tariq replied.

"I was a free member of the Keita clan of the Malinke of Mali," Kankan replied with pride and indignation.

"You don't know who you are," said Tariq.

"I bought your freedom with gold," Tariq was saying. "I offered you a camel, but you chose to walk like a slave. Already, you think like a slave. Here in the desert, where death is near, I offer you shelter, food, and water—life—and you think only of slitting my throat when my back is turned. You claim to be a man, but you have not yet mastered the beast within you."

Kankan found himself at a loss for what to do or say.

"Sit," Tariq said. "Sit and eat. The journey is long, but it can only be made one step at a time."

Kankan sat down but did not finish his meal right away. "Where are you going?" he asked.

"Where I am going is of less importance to you than where I have been," Tariq said. "The question is, Where are you going?"

"I want to return home to my village," Kankan said.

Tariq shook his head slowly. "you have only just begun your journey. It would not be good to turn back now. You must go on."

"Where? Kankan asked.

"I cannot tell you where. Only Allah knows. But if you will be guided by him, then I will journey with you awhile. There is much that I can share with you that may help you to discover Il-Rah—the Way, the Path. You have only begun to be tested."

During his life Mansa Musa was famous for his great wealth and power. However, by 1490, Mali's place as the most powerful kingdom in western Africa had been taken over by the Kingdom of Songhai.

Source: Khephra, Burns, *Mansa Musa*. San Diego: Gulliver Books, Harcourt, Inc., 2001.

Tale of King Arthur

Retold by James Knowles, 1923

One of the best-known tales of the Middle Ages, a period in Europe from about A.D. 500 to 1500, involves a king of England named Arthur. According to legend, King Arthur lived in the A.D. 400s. The tale of King Arthur, which has been told over and over again for hundreds of years, concerns heroic deeds, tragic love stories, and magical powers. In the excerpt below, a wizard named Merlin has cast a magic spell and taken young Arthur away from his father, King Uther. A knight named Sir Ector has then raised Arthur as his own son. As you read this excerpt, notice the amazing feat that Arthur performs to become king. According to the storyteller, what were the qualities that made a great leader in the Middle Ages?

Now Arthur the prince had all this time been nourished in Sir Ector's house as his own son, and was fair and tall and **comely**, being of the age of fifteen years, great in strength, gentle in manner, and accomplished in all exercises proper for the training of a knight.

comely: attractive

But as yet he knew not of his father; for Merlin [the magician] had so dealt, that none save Uther and himself knew **aught** about [Arthur]. Wherefore it **befell**, that many of the knights and barons who heard King Uther speak before his death, and call his son Arthur his successor, were in great amazement; and some doubted, and others were displeased.

aught: anything
befell: happened

Anon the chief lords and princes set forth each to his own land, and, raising armed men and **multitudes** of followers, determined every one to gain the crown for himself; for they said in their hearts, "If there be any such a son at all as he of whom this wizard forced the king to speak, who are we that a beardless boy should have rule over us?"

anon: soon
multitudes: crowds

So the land stood long in great peril, for every lord and baron sought but his own advantage; and the **Saxons**, growing ever more adventurous, wasted and overran the towns and villages in every part.

Saxons: Germanic tribe that conquered parts of England in the fifth century

Then Merlin went to Brice, the **Archbishop of Canterbury**, and advised him to require all the earls and barons of the **realm** and all knights and gentlemen-at-arms to come to him at London, before Christmas, that they might learn the will of Heaven who should be king. This, therefore, the archbishop did, and upon Christmas Eve were met together in London all the greatest princes, lords, and barons; and . . . the archbishop **besought** Heaven for a sign who should be lawful king of all the realm.

And as they prayed, there was seen in the churchyard, set straight before the doorways of the church, a huge square stone having a naked sword stuck in the midst of it. And on the sword was written in letters of gold, "Whoso pulleth out the sword from this stone is born the rightful King of Britain."

At this all the people wondered greatly; and, when [the religious service] was over, the nobles, knights, and princes ran out eagerly from the church to see the stone and sword; and a law was **forthwith** made that whoso should pull out the sword should be **acknowledged straightway** King of Britain.

Then many knights and barons pulled at the sword with all their might, and some of them tried many times, but none could stir or move it.

When all had tried in vain, the archbishop declared the man whom Heaven had chosen was not yet here. "But God," said he, "will doubtless make him known **ere** many days."

So ten knights were chosen, being men of **high renown**, to watch and keep the sword; and there was proclamation made through all the land that whosoever would, had leave and liberty to try and pull it from the stone. But though great multitudes of people came, both gentle and simple, for many days, no man could ever move the sword a hair's **breadth** from its place.

Now, at the New Year's Eve a great tournament was to be held in London. . . .To which tournament there came, with many other knights, Sir Ector, Arthur's foster-father, who had great possessions near to London; and with him came his son, Sir Key, but recently made knight, to take his part in the **jousting**, and young Arthur also to witness all the sports and fighting.

But as they rode towards the jousts, Sir Key found suddenly he had no sword, for he had left it at his father's house; and turning to young Arthur, he prayed him to ride back and fetch it for him. "I will with a good will," said Arthur; and rode fast back after the sword.

But when he came to the house he found it locked and empty, for all were gone forth to see the tournament. Whereat, being angry and impatient, he said within himself, "I will ride to the churchyard and take with me the sword that sticketh in the stone, for my brother shall not go without a sword this day."

So he rode and came to the churchyard, and **alighting** from his horse he tied him to the gate, and went to the **pavilion**, which was

archbishop of Canterbury: important leader of the Church of England

realm: kingdom

besought: begged

forthwith: immediately

acknowledged: recognized

straightway: right away

ere: before

high renown: great fame

breadth: width

jousting: competition in which knights carrying spears charge at each other on horseback

alighting: getting off

pavilion: large tent

pitched near the stone, wherein **abode** the ten knights who watched and kept it; but he found no knights there, for all were gone to see the jousting.

abode: stayed

Then he took the sword by its handle, and lightly and fiercely he pulled it out of the stone, and took his horse and rode until he came to Sir Key and delivered him the sword. But as soon as Sir Key saw it he knew well it was the sword of the stone, and riding swiftly to his father, he cried out, "Lo! here, sir, is the sword of the stone, wherefore it is I who must be king of all this land."

When Sir Ector saw the sword, he turned back straight with Arthur and Sir Key and came to the churchyard, and there alighting, they went all three into the church, and Sir Key was sworn to tell truly how he came by the sword. Then he confessed it was his brother Arthur who had brought it to him.

Whereat Sir Ector, turning to young Arthur, asked him—"How gottest thou the sword?"

"Sir," said he, "I will tell you. When I went home to fetch my brother's sword, I found nobody to deliver it to me, for all were **abroad** to the jousts. Yet was I **loth** to leave my brother swordless, and **bethinking me** of this one, I came **hither** eagerly to fetch it for him, and pulled it out of the stone without any pain."

abroad: gone
loth: reluctant
bethinking me: thinking
hither: to this place

Then said Sir Ector, much amazed and looking **steadfastly** on Arthur, "If this indeed be thus, 'tis thou who shalt be king of all this

steadfastly: firmly

land—and God will have it so—for none but he who should be rightful Lord of Britain might ever draw this sword forth from that stone. But let me now with mine own eyes see thee put back the sword into its place and draw it forth again."

"That is no mystery," said Arthur; and straightway set it in the stone. And then Sir Ector pulled at it himself, and after him Sir Key, with all his might, but both of them in vain: then Arthur reaching forth his hand and grasping at the **pommel**, pulled it out easily, and at once.

pommel: knob on the handle

Then fell Sir Ector down upon his knees upon the ground before young Arthur, and Sir Key also with him, and straightway did him **homage** as their **sovereign** lord.

homage: honor
sovereign: supreme

But Arthur cried aloud, "Alas! mine own dear father and my brother, why kneel ye thus to me?"

"Nay, my Lord Arthur," answered then Sir Ector, "we are of no blood-kinship with thee, and little though I thought how high thy kin might be, yet wast thou never more than foster-child of mine." And then he told him all he knew about his infancy, and how a stranger had delivered him, with a great sum of gold, into his hands to be brought up and nourished as his own born child, and then had disappeared.

But when young Arthur heard of it, he fell upon Sir Ector's neck, and wept, and made great **lamentation**, "For now," said he, "I have in one day lost my father and my mother and my brother."

lamentation: wailing

"Sir," said Sir Ector presently, "when thou shalt be made king be good and gracious unto me and mine."

"If not," said Arthur, "I were no true man's son at all, for thou art he in all the world to whom I owe the most; and my good lady and mother, thy wife, hath ever kept and fostered me as though I were her own; so if it be God's will that I be king hereafter as thou sayest, [ask] of me whatever thing thou wilt and I will do it; and God forbid that I should fail thee in it."

"I will but pray," replied Sir Ector, "that thou wilt make my son Sir Key, thy foster-brother, **seneschal** of all the lands."

seneschal: agent in charge

"That shall he be," said Arthur, "and never shall another hold that office, save thy son, while he and I do live."

Anon they left the church and went to the archbishop to tell him that the sword had been achieved. And when he saw the sword in Arthur's hand he set a day and **summoned** all the princes, knights, and barons to meet again at St. Paul's Church and see the will of Heaven **signified**. So when they came together, the sword was put back in the stone, and all tried, from the greatest to the least, to move it; but there before them all not one could take it out **save** Arthur only.

summoned: sent for

signified: fulfilled

save: except

Throughout the centuries, the legend of King Arthur has been retold in novels, poetry, plays, operas, and films. Other versions of the tale of King Arthur focus on great battles, epic quests, or searches, and the legendary Knights of the Round Table.

Source: Sir James Knowles, compiler, *King Arthur and His Knights*. New York: Blue Ribbon Books, 1923.

CONTRACT BETWEEN A VASSAL AND LORD Agreement from the 600s

During the Middle Ages, many Europeans lived in fear of attack from invaders and from each other. To protect themselves, Europeans developed a system known as feudalism. Under feudalism people provided certain services to each other in exchange for protection. Kings granted large estates to nobles, or lords, who promised to defend the king's territory. In turn the lords made contracts with less powerful nobles called vassals. When a vassal and lord exchanged vows, they often marked the occasion with a grand ceremony. Below is a standard contract between vassal and lord dating from the 7th century. As you read this contract, notice what vassal and lord promise each other. What do you think are some of the benefits and drawbacks of taking such an oath for both lord and vassal?

VASSAL:

I _____ , Since it is known familiarly to all how little I have **whence** to feed and clothe myself, I have therefore **petitioned** your **Piety**, and your good will has permitted me to hand myself over or commend myself to your **guardianship**, which I have thereupon done; that is to say, in this way, that you should aid and **succor** me as well with food as with clothing, according as I shall be able to serve you and deserve it.

And so long as I shall live I ought to provide service and honor to you, suitably to my free condition; and I . . . must remain during the days of my life under your power or defense.

whence: with which
petitioned: sought help from
Piety: Lordship
guardianship: care
succor: help

LORD:

It is right that those who offer to us unbroken **fidelity** should be protected by our aid. And since _____ , a faithful one of ours, by the favor of God, coming here in our palace with his arms, has seen fit to swear trust and fidelity to us in our hand, therefore we herewith **decree** and command that for the future _____ , above mentioned, be **reckoned** among the number of the **antrustions**.

fidelity: loyalty

decree: order
reckoned: counted
antrustions: followers

Life in Europe during the Middle Ages was often harsh and brutal, especially for serfs— the least powerful members of feudal society—who lived and worked on the land belonging to the nobles. Unlike the lords and vassals, serfs were not protected by any written contracts. Serfs had to follow the rules of the nobles.

Source: James Harvey Robinson, *Readings in European History*, Volume 1. Boston: Athenaeum, 1904.

Notebooks from the Renaissance

by Leonardo da Vinci, about 1482–1519

From about 1350 to 1600, Europe witnessed a rebirth of art, learning, and culture known as the Renaissance. No one embodied the spirit of the Renaissance more than Leonardo da Vinci (1452–1519). An Italian artist, scientist, and inventor, Leonardo studied every part of nature to better understand the world around him. Throughout his life da Vinci kept notebooks in which he sketched drawings and jotted down ideas. Da Vinci, who was left-handed, wrote backward from right to left so that his handwriting can only be read by holding it up to a mirror. As you read the selections and look at the drawings from da Vinci's notebooks, think about how his drawing and ideas capture the spirit of the Renaissance. In what ways was da Vinci a person far ahead of his time?

A Man when running throws less weight on his legs than when standing still. And in the same way a horse which is running feels less the weight of the man he carries. Hence many persons think it wonderful that in running, the horse can rest on one single foot.

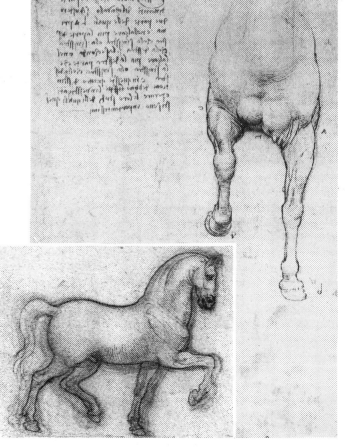

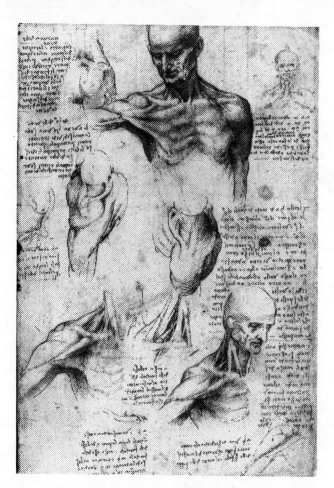

Give the measurement of each muscle, and give the reasons of all their functions, and in which they work and what makes them work. . . . First draw the spine of the back; then clothe it by degrees, one after the other, with each of its muscles and put in the nerves and arteries and veins to each muscle by itself; and besides these note the vertebrae to which they are attached; which of the intestines come in contact with them; and which bones and other organs. . . .

A Bird is an instrument working according to mathematical law, which instrument it is in the capacity of man to reproduce. . . . A man with wings large enough and [properly] attached might learn to overcome the resistance of the air . . . and raise himself upon it. Remember that your bird must imitate no other than the bat, because its membranes serve as . . . the frame of the wings. . . . [Take apart] the bat and on this model arrange the machine. . . .

Nature is [taken in] through the senses, mainly through the sense of sight. The art of painting is [part of] the process of seeing. . . . . The painter must analyze this experience in order to reproduce the visual image appearing in the eye on his picture place. His painting should give the impression of a window through which we look out into a section·of the visible world. . . . The mind of a painter should be like a mirror, which always takes the color of the object it reflects and is filled by the images of as many objects as are in front of it. Therefore you must know that you cannot be a good painter unless you . . . represent by your art every kind of form produced by nature.

Leonardo da Vinci is remembered today for some of his great paintings, such as the Mona Lisa *and* The Last Supper. *He is also remembered for his great sketches and ideas for inventions. Many of these inventions—such as the airplane—were so advanced that they could not actually be built for hundreds of years after da Vinci's death.*

Source: Irma A. Richter, ed., *Selections from the Notebooks of Leonardo de Vinci:* Oxford University Press, 1952.

The Splendors of Hangzhou

by an Unknown Chinese Traveler, 1235

For thousands of years cities have been an important part of Chinese life. One of the oldest cities in China is Hangzhou (HAHNG joh). This city along the east coast of China served as the nation's capital in the twelfth and thirteenth centuries. During this period Hangzhou overflowed with markets, goods, and endless types of entertainment. The drawing on the next page, which was created by a Chinese artist living in Hangzhou during the 1200s, shows one of the city's many silk shops. In 1235 a Chinese traveler visited this fascinating city and described its attractions. As you read this traveler's account, think of what you might do if you had one day to spend in ancient Hangzhou. How do the attractions of thirteenth-century Hangzhou compare with attractions of cities today?

Markets

In the evening, with the exception of the square in front of the palace, the markets are as busy as during the day. The most attractive one is at Central Square, where all sorts of **exquisite artifacts**, instruments, containers, and hundreds of varieties of goods are for sale. In other marketplaces, sales, auctions, and exchanges go on constantly. In the wine shops and inns business also thrives. Only after the fourth drum does the city gradually quiet down, but by the fifth drum, court officials already start preparing for audiences and merchants are getting ready for the morning market again. This cycle goes on all year round without **respite**. . . .

exquisite artifacts: beautiful hand-crafted goods

respite: rest

Commercial Establishments

Various businesses are designated by the word "company" (*hang*), which is a taxation category **imposed** by the government and is used for all businesses dealing in **commodities**, regardless of their size. Even physicians and fortunetellers are included. Other trades sometimes also borrow the word "company" for their own use, such as liquor company and food company. Some businesses are called "gatherings" (*ho*), such as a flower gathering, fruit gathering, dried-fish gathering. . . . **Artisans** sometimes call their businesses "workshops" (*tso*), such as comb workshop, belt workshop, gold-and-silver plating workshop. There are some businesses that use unusual names; for example, shops dealing in the "seven treasures" (gold, silver, pearl, amber, etc.) may call themselves **curio** companies, whereas a bathhouse may be designated a fragrant-water company.

imposed: set up
commodities: goods

artisans: skilled workers

curio: rare goods

In general, the capital attracts the greatest variety of goods and has the best craftsmen. For instance, the flower company at Superior Lane does a truly excellent job of flower arrangement, and its caps, hairpins, and collars are **unsurpassed** in craftsmanship. Some of the most famous specialties of the capital are the sweet-bean soup at the **Miscellaneous** **Market**, the pickled dates of the Ko family, the thick soup of the Kuang family at Superior Lane, the fruit at the Great Commons marketplace, the cooked meats in front of Eternal Mercy Temple, Sister Sung's fish broth at Penny Pond Gate, the juicy lungs at Flowing Gold Gate, the "lamb rice" of the Chih family at Central Square, the boots of the P'eng family, the fine clothing of the Hsüan family at Southern Commons, the sticky rice pastry of the Chang family, the flutes made by Ku the Fourth, and the Ch'iu family's Tatar whistles at the Great Commons. . . .

unsurpassed: not topped

miscellaneous: varied

Entertainment Centers

The hundred games used to be the official entertainment of the old capital. The experts . . . can climb high poles, do somersaults, walk on stilts, juggle spears . . . play with swords, display horsemanship, and so on.

The various skills of the entertainers have their respective high-sounding names. Their acts include: kicking bottles, juggling plates, kicking musical stones, twirling drumsticks, kicking writing brushes, playing ball. There are also performances with trained insects, fish or bears, fireworks, fire shows, water shows, puppet shows, and marksmanship of all kinds.

Puppet shows include string-puppets, cane-top puppets, water-puppets, and flesh-puppets. The stories are usually fictitious and fantastic. Shadow plays originated in the old capital. At first the figures were made with white paper; later they were made of leather and painted various colors. The stories of the shadow plays are pretty much the same

71

as those used by the storytellers; generally speaking, they are a mixture of truth and fiction. The loyal and righteous are given a handsome appearance, whereas the wicked and **treacherous** are depicted as monstrously ugly—a kind of **implicit** criticism that is easily understood by the people in the streets. The storytellers can be divided into four groups: those who specialize in social tales, mysteries, and miracle tales; those who deal with military adventures; those who **explicate sutras** by telling religious tales; and those who relate historical events. . . .

treacherous: untrustworthy

implicit: understood

explicate: explain
sutras: sacred Buddhist teachings

Boats

The capital is encircled by a river on the left side and by West Lake on the right; thus the most convenient way to travel is by boat. The boats for hire on West Lake vary greatly in size. Some are 50 feet [15 m] long and have a capacity of more than 100 passengers; others are 20 to 30 feet [6 to 9 m] long and can take 30 to 50 passengers. All of them are exquisitely constructed, with carvings on the railings and paintings on the beams. They sail so smoothly that the passengers may forget that they are on water. These boats are for hire in all seasons and never lack patrons. They are also well equipped with everything; a tourist can get on board in the morning, drink wine, and enjoy himself; at dusk he may walk home by following a trail. It is not tiring but is rather expensive. Some wealthy families have their own pleasure boats, and these are even more exquisitely built and more luxuriously fitted out.

Dragon boat competitions are held in spring at the West Lake and in autumn at the Che River. The dragon boats are light and swift and make a grand **spectacle**. . . . In early and mid-autumn there are swimmers in the Che River, who, **brandishing** pennants and poles, display the most breathtaking skills. I believe this is a unique attraction of the capital. . . .

spectacle: show
brandishing: waving

Specialty Stores

Some famous fabric stores sell exquisite brocade and fine silk which are unsurpassed elsewhere in the country. Along the river, close to the Peaceful Ford Bridge, there are numerous fabric stores, fan shops, and **lacquerware** and porcelain shops. Most other cities can only boast of one special product; what makes the capital unique is that it gathers goods from all places. Furthermore, because of the large population and busy commercial traffic, there is a demand for everything. There are even shops that deal exclusively in used paper or in feathers, for instance.

lacquerware: varnished wood products

The treasures of Hangzhou and other parts of China were among the greatest in the world. After Marco Polo visited China in the late 1200s, tales of China's wealth began to spread to Europe. Europeans wanted these fabulous goods and luxuries, and a busy trade soon flourished. During the 1400s Europeans, who were eager for such treasures, began racing to find the shortest route to China and Asia.

Source: Patricia Buckley Ebrey, ed., *Chinese Civilization and Society*. New York: The Free Press, 1981.

The Tale of Genji

by Murasaki Shikibu, early 1000s

In the late tenth century, Japanese literature began to flower with stories and poems about the rituals and ceremonies of the island nation's palace life. Around the year 1000 Murasaki Shikibu (moor uh SAHK ee SHEE kee boo, 978–1031), a woman who worked for the empress, wrote Genji monogatari, *which translates as* The Tale of Genji (GEN JEE). *This book, often considered the world's first novel, is about the adventures of a prince named Genji and numbers more than 4,000 pages. In the following excerpt the prince gets caught in a dangerous storm while he is away from the emperor's palace. What does this story tell you about the customs and beliefs of Japanese society in the eleventh century?*

It was the day of the serpent, the first such day in the Third Month. "The day when a man who has worries goes down and washes them away," said one of his men, admirably informed, it would seem, in all the **annual observances**.

annual observances: yearly ceremonies

Wishing to have a look at the seashore, Genji set forth. Plain, rough curtains were strung up among the trees, and a **soothsayer** who was doing the circuit of the province was **summoned** to perform the **lustration**.

soothsayer: fortune teller

summoned: called

lustration: purifying ceremony

Genji thought he could see something of himself in the rather large doll being cast off to sea, bearing away sins and **tribulations**. . . .

tribulations: sufferings

The bright open seashore showed him to wonderful advantage. The sea stretched placid into **measureless** distances. He thought of all that had happened to him, and all that was still to come. . . .

measureless: great

Suddenly a wind came up and even before the services were finished the sky was black. Genji's men rushed about in confusion. Rain came pouring down, completely without warning. Though the obvious course would have been to return **straightway** to the house, there had been no time to send for umbrellas. The wind was now a howling **tempest**, everything that had not been tied down was **scuttling** off across the beach. The surf was biting at their feet. The sea was white, as if spread over with white linen. Lightning flashed and thunder roared. Fearful every moment of being struck down, they finally made their way back to the house.

straightway: at once

tempest: storm

scuttling: scurrying

"I've never seen anything like it," said one of the men. "Winds do come up from time to time, but not without warning. It is all very strange and very terrible."

The lightning and thunder seemed to announce the end of the world, and the rain to beat its way into the ground; and Genji sat calmly reading a **sutra**. The thunder **subsided** in the evening, but the wind went on through the night.

"Our prayers seem to have been answered. A little more and we would have been carried off. I've heard that tidal waves do carry people off before they know what is happening to them, but I've not seen anything like this.". . .

sutra: sacred Buddhist teaching
subsided: lessened

Genji offered prayers to the king of the sea and countless other gods as well. The thunder was increasingly more terrible, and finally the gallery adjoining his rooms was struck by lightning. Flames sprang up and the gallery was destroyed. The confusion was immense; the whole world seemed to have gone mad. Genji was moved to a building out in back, a kitchen or something of the sort it seemed to be. It was crowded with people of every station and rank. The **clamor** was almost enough to drown out the lightning and thunder. Night descended over a sky already as black as ink.

clamor: noise

Presently the wind and rain subsided and stars began to come out. The kitchen being altogether too mean a place, a move back to the main hall was suggested. The **charred** remains of the gallery were an ugly sight, however, and the hall had been badly muddied and all the blinds and curtains blown away. . . .

charred: burned

[Genji] opened a **wattled** door and looked out. The moon had come up. The line left by the waves was white and dangerously near, and the surf was still high. There was no one here whom he could turn to, no student of the deeper truths who could **discourse** upon past and present and perhaps explain these wild events. All the fisherfolk had gathered at what they had heard was the house of a great gentleman from the city. They were as noisy and impossible to communicate with as a flock of birds, but no one thought of telling them to leave.

wattled: woven with poles and reeds

discourse: talk

"If the wind had kept up just a little longer," someone said, "absolutely everything would have been swept under. The gods did well by us."

Genji goes through many adventures before this 11th-century novel comes to a close. In addition to writing this novel, Murasaki Shikibu also kept a diary that reveals much about life in ancient Japan.

Source: Murasaki Shikibu, *The Tale of Genji*. New York: Vintage Books, 1990.

THE WORLD EXPANDS AND CHANGES

We have already seen the light. . . . The chains have been broken, we have been freed.

Simón Bolívar, 1815

The Legacy Of Columbus

by Sarah Elder Hale, 1992

When Christopher Columbus (1451–1506) came to the Americas in 1492, the land that was the "New World" to him was an old world to the cultures that had lived there over the past 10,000 years. The following selection is an editorial that was written on the 500th anniversary of Columbus's arrival in the Americas. As the author points out, without that time of change and exchange between cultures, we would not have the diverse cultural heritage we enjoy today. What things in your daily life came from other cultures? How has the world changed since the time of Columbus?

Most of you know that 1992 marks the five hundredth anniversary, the quincentennial, of Christopher Columbus's voyage across the "Ocean Sea" and his arrival in what was later called the Americas. Columbus's mission was to find a westward route to the rich lands of India, the Spice Islands, Cipangu (Japan), and other Asian ports and to carry with him the message of Christianity. He did not know that two continents lay between him and Asia. His accidental "discovery" of lands and peoples unknown to Europeans changed the world.

In 1492, Columbus started an exhange of cultures, resources, and ideas that continues to this day. Food, animals, customs, and diseases crisscrossed the Atlantic in the years following Columbus's first voyage. Unfortunately, the native peoples suffered greatly under Spanish **colonialism**. It was a dramatic encounter between two civilizations, an encounter that changed forever the course of history.

colonialism: conquering

We use the words "change" and "exchange" often in history. Without change, we could not further our understanding of the world around us, and without exchange, cultures would become **isolated** and **stagnant**. In 1992, every American should take time to reflect on what Columbus's voyage has meant to this country and the world. Some will celebrate the **intermingling** of cultures; others will protest these celebrations and mourn what was lost when Columbus landed in America. But we also should look ahead. What will people's understanding of the world (or the universe) be five hundred years from now, and what will historians think of those who lived in 1992?

isolated: separate

stagnant: inactive and unchanging

intermingling: mixing

Both the European and Native American cultures have given us traditions that still exist today. The Americas—especially the United States—continue to become more and more culturally diverse as we communicate and trade with people in all parts of the world, and as people immigrate. In what ways do you think the world may change in the next 500 years?

Source: *Cobblestone Magazine* (January, Vol. 13, No. 1). Peterborough, NH: Cobblestone Publishing, Inc., 1992.

BATTLE OF TENOCHTITLÁN

by Aztec Historians, 1521

Beginning around 1325, the Aztec ruled a powerful empire in the Central Valley of Mexico. In 1519, however, Hernando Cortéz and his army of Spanish soldiers arrived in the Aztec capital of Tenochtitlán. At first the Aztec ruler Moctezuma permitted the Spaniards to enter the city peacefully. The Spaniards, however, were not interested in peace but rather in the vast quantities of Aztec gold and silver stored at Tenochtitlán. The Spaniards attacked the Aztec and, in 1521, laid siege to the city for 85 days. Aztec historians recorded these events in pictographs, a form of writing in which pictures are used to represent events and ideas. Aztec pictographs were written on amatl (ah MAHT ul), a type of paper that was made by pounding the inner bark of a wild fig tree. The pictograph on the next page, based on the Aztec calendar, tells the history of the Spanish conquest. The three boxes at the top of the pictograph contain Aztec symbols that stand for three different years. Study the other images and try to determine what they mean. Then compare your ideas to the explanation below.

On the left side of the pictograph, the soldier on a horse carrying a sword, shield, and cross represents the Spaniards landing in Mexico in the Aztec year of 1-Reed. It is believed that the event in this picture took place in 1519, because a reed, which is pictured in the box above the soldier, is one of the symbols used by Aztecs in naming that year. The Aztecs used a calendar year fixed at 365 days, much as the United States and many other countries do today.

Beside the Spanish soldier is an Aztec official who is greeting him. The official is shown offering the soldier a gift, which indicates that at first the Aztecs welcomed the Spaniards. The faces in the row of images at the bottom of the pictograph show the different Indian groups allied with the Aztecs.

The next scene shows that during the year of 2-Flint, or 1520, a fight took place in the Aztec capital. The pictograph shows Aztec priests being cut down in battle by the Spaniards' steel swords on the steps of the city's main pyramid. This pyramid—the most important building in Tenochtitlán—housed the two main temples dedicated to Aztec gods. These are shown by the two sets of steps leading up the pyramid. Try to find the image of the cactus and stone joined to a temple, which was another symbol for Tenochtitlán. Although the Spaniards' first attempt to capture Tenochtitlán was unsuccessful, they later conquered the city on the day 1-Serpent of the year 3-House, or 1521.

After defeating the Aztec at Tenochtitlán, the Spaniards built a new city, called Mexico City, on top of the Aztec ruins. Today Mexico City is the capital of Mexico. This pictograph preserves the memory of Tenochtitlán and helps us to understand the Spanish conquest from an Aztec point of view. Suppose you were asked to make a pictograph of an event in your life or that of your classroom or country. What symbols might you use?

TEARS OF THE INDIANS

by Bartolomé de Las Casas, 1542

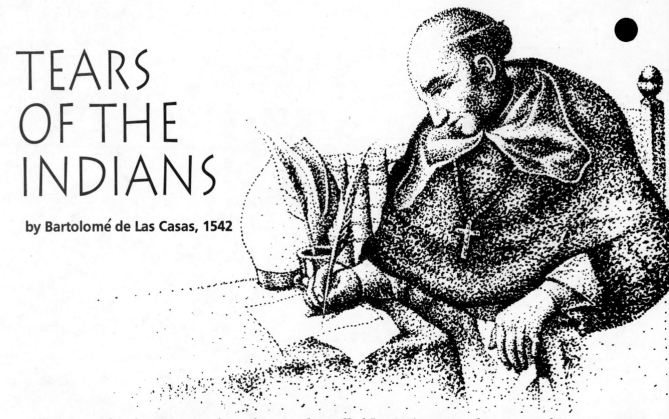

When Spanish colonists arrived in what is today called Latin America, they set up the encomienda system, which used enslaved Indians as forced labor. This system, as well as the diseases brought by Europeans, caused the deaths of many Native Americans in the early 1500s. Bartolomé de las Casas (1474–1566) was a Spanish priest who supported the encomienda system at first but then turned against it. In fact, Las Casas was so upset about the behavior of the Spanish colonists that he wrote letters to Spain's rulers, protesting the mistreatment of Indians. In the excerpt below, translated from a book he wrote in 1542 about the colonies, Las Casas presents his views about how the Spaniards' actions were destroying the Indians and their civilization. According to Las Casas, what effect did Spanish colonization have on the Indians? What evidence does he give to support his claim?

There were ten kingdoms [on the continent of North America] as large as the kingdom of Spain, Aragon, and Portugal, **encompassing** over a thousand square miles [2,600 sq km]. Of all this the inhumane and **abominable** villainies of the Spaniards have made a wilderness, for though it was formerly occupied by vast and **infinite** numbers of men [women and children] it is stripped of all people. And we dare assert with confidence that in those forty years during which the Spaniards have exercised their abominable cruelties and detestable **tyrannies** in those parts, over twelve million souls innocently **perished**, women and children being included in the sad and fatal list. Moreover I truly believe that I should be speaking within the truth if I were to say that over fifty millions were **consumed** in this massacre.

encompassing: including

abominable: terrible

infinite: endless

tyrannies: abuses of power

perished: died

consumed: killed

As for those that came out of Spain, boasting themselves to be Christians, they had two ways of **extirpating** the Indian nation from the face of the earth: the first was by making bloody, unjust, and cruel wars against them, the second was by killing all those that so much as sought to recover their liberty, as some of the braver sort did. And as for the women and children that were left alive, the Spaniards laid so heavy and **grievous** a **yoke of servitude** upon them that the condition of beasts was much more tolerable.

All the various other torments and inhumanities which they **employed** to the ruin of these poor nations may be included under these two headings.

What led the Spaniards to these **unsanctified impieties** was the desire for gold to make themselves suddenly rich, in order to obtain dignities and honors that were in no way fit for them. In a word their **covetousness**, their ambition which could not be exceeded by any people under heaven, the riches of the country, and the patience of the people gave occasion for this devilish **barbarism**. For the Spaniards so despised them (I now speak what I have seen without the least untruth) that they used them not like beasts, for that would have been tolerable, but looked upon them as if they had been but the **dung** and filth of the earth, and so little did they regard the health of their souls that they permitted this great **multitude** to die without the least light of religion. Nor is this less true than what I have said before and what those tyrants and hangmen themselves do not deny . . . namely, that the Indians never gave them the least cause for such violence but received them as angels sent from heaven, until the excessive cruelties and torments and slaughters moved them to take arms against the Spaniards. . . .

extirpating: wiping out

grievous: painful
yoke of servitude: state of slavery

employed: used

unsanctified impieties: wicked deeds

covetousness: greed

barbarism: uncivilized acts

dung: manure

multitude: large number

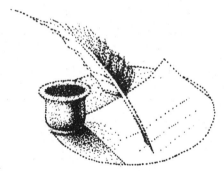

During the early 1500s Bartolomé de Las Casas's voice of protest was heard by the Spanish king. In 1516 Las Casas was appointed "Protector of the Indians." He made the cause of protecting the rights of Indians his lifelong crusade. Due to Las Casas's efforts, the New Laws—royal decrees prohibiting forced labor of the Indians—were issued in 1542, the same year his book appeared. But the Spaniards soon replaced the Indians with enslaved people from Africa.

Source: Adapted from the translation by John Phillips, from Bartolomé de Las Casas, *The Tears of the Indians, Being an Historical and True Account of the Cruel Massacres and Slaughters of above Twenty Millions of Innocent People* (London, 1656), in Charles Gibson, ed., *The Spanish Tradition in America.* New York: Harper, 1968.

CAPTURED!

by Olaudah Equiano, 1789

When Europeans arrived in Africa in the late 1400s, they greatly expanded the slave trade that Arab merchants had been carrying on for hundreds of years. They also began to forcibly transport Africans overseas to the Americas. In 1756 Olaudah Equiano (AHL uh duh ih kwee AH nah, 1745–1797) was an 11-year-old boy living in the village of Benin in what is today Nigeria. One day slave traders came to his village and changed his life forever. In his autobiography Equiano described this fateful day and what happened afterward. As you read the following excerpt from his autobiography, think of the experiences he describes. How does he manage to endure?

One day, when all our people were gone out to their works as usual, and only I and my dear sister were left to mind the house, two men and a woman got over our walls, and in a moment seized us both; and, without giving us time to cry out, or make resistance, they **stopped** our mouths, and ran off with us into the nearest wood. Here they tied our hands, and continued to carry us as far as they could, till night came on, when we reached a small house, where the robbers halted for refreshment, and spent the night. We were then unbound; but were unable to take any food; and, being quite overpowered by fatigue and grief, our only relief was some sleep, which **allayed** our misfortune for a short time.

stopped: stuffed something into

allayed: eased

The next morning we left the house, and continued travelling all the day. For a long time we had kept [to] the woods, but at last we came into a road which I believed I knew. I had now some hopes of being **delivered**; for we had advanced but a little way before I discovered some people at a distance, [and] I began to cry out for their assistance; but my cries had no other effect than to make them tie me [tighter] and stop my mouth, and then they put me into a large sack. They also stopped my sister's mouth, and tied her hands; and in this manner we proceeded till we were out of the sight of these people.

delivered: rescued

When we went to rest the following night they offered us some **victuals**; but we refused them; and the only comfort we had was in being in one another's arms all that night, and bathing each other with our tears. But alas! We were soon deprived of even the smallest comfort of weeping together. The next day proved a day of greater sorrow than I had yet experienced; for my sister and I were then separated, while we lay clasped in each other's arms: it was in vain that we **besought** them not to part us: she was torn from me, and immediately carried away, while I was left in a state of **distraction** not to be described. I cried and grieved continually; and for several days did not eat any thing but what they forced into my mouth. . . .

victuals: food

besought: begged

distraction: worry

From the time I left my own nation I always found somebody that understood me till I came to the sea coast. The languages of different nations did not totally differ, nor were they so **copious** as those of the Europeans, particularly the English. They were therefore easily learned; and, while I was journeying thus through Africa, I **acquired** two or three different **tongues**.

copious: full of words

acquired: learned
tongues: languages

In this manner I had been travelling for a considerable time, when one evening, to my great surprise, whom should I see brought to the house where I was but my dear sister? As soon as she saw me she gave a loud shriek, and ran into my arms—I was quite overpowered: neither of us could speak, but, for a considerable time, clung to each other in mutual embraces, unable to do any thing but weep. Our meeting affected all who saw us; and indeed I must acknowledge, in honour of those **sable** destroyers of human rights, that I never met with any ill treatment, or saw any offered to their slaves, except tying them, when necessary, to keep them from running away. When these people knew we were brother and sister, they **indulged** us to be together; . . . and thus for a while we forgot our misfortunes in the joy of being together; but even this small comfort was soon to have an end; for scarcely had the **fatal** morning appeared, when she was again torn from me forever! I was now more miserable, if possible, than before. . . .

sable: dark

indulged: allowed

fatal: dreaded

I continued to travel, sometimes by land, sometimes by water, through different countries, and various nations, till, at the end of six or seven months after I had been kidnapped I arrived at the sea coast.

After arriving on the west coast of Africa, Olaudah Equiano was sold to European slave traders. They transported him overseas to Barbados. Equiano was one of more than 14 million Africans captured and carried by force to the Americas from the late 1400s to the 1800s. Equiano, however, was more fortunate than most. A British sea captain later bought him and made him a sailor. Although enslaved, Equiano managed to earn money and bought his freedom in 1766. As a free man, he traveled the world and explored the northern Arctic. Years later he settled in England and wrote his autobiography. The book was widely read in the 1790s and helped the growth of the antislavery movement.

Source: Olaudah Equiano, *The Interesting Narrative of the Life of Olaudah Equiano, or Gustavus Vassa, the African. Written by Himself*. London: W. Durell, 1791.

Stowaway

by Karen Hesse

Captain James Cook was an 18th century British naval explorer, who made three important voyages of discovery between 1768 and 1779. He was the commander of the Endeavour during an expedition to the South Pacific that began in 1768. The purpose of this voyage was to observe the planet Venus as it eclipsed the sun. Scientists accompanied him on the journey. In April 1769 the Endeavour reached the island of Tahiti in the southern Pacific Ocean. Then it sailed around New Zealand and the east coast of Australia before returning to England in June of 1771. This selection is a fictionalized diary written by Nicholas Young, an eleven year old stowaway on board the ship. Although the diary was made up by the author of the book, the events described really took place. As you read this excerpt, think about what it was like to explore the South Pacific more than two centuries ago before the invention of modern navigational tools and computers. How do you think this young boy felt as he hid on board the ship? What was it like for him to be so far from home?

August 1768
Sunday 7th to Friday 19th {Plymouth}

    With the help of seamen Francis Haite, John Ramsey, and Samuel Evans, I have managed to keep my presence aboard *Endeavour* secret. She's a small **Bark**, and her company over eighty in number. It's a wonder I've not been discovered, with all the coming and going of the men aboard, but I have not. The three seamen I paid to get me on bring biscuits and water. They make certain I exercise each night during middle watch, when there are fewer hands on deck. But there is little to relieve my situation till *Endeavour* sails.

Bark: a 3-masted ship

    It's a good hiding place I've got, in the **aft** of what Samuel Evans calls the **Pinnace**, a small boat *Endeavour* carries aboard her. I can look over the edge and see the deck without being noticed. But it is difficult, lying still, day and night. Sometimes the urge to cry out nearly gets the better of me. I haven't yet. It would go hard on the men who have helped me if I did. And I would be returned to the Butcher, who would take it out of my hide, if father didn't kill me first.

aft: the stern or rear part of a ship
Pinnace: light sailing ship

Endeavour creaks without rest as she sits at anchor. The breeze chatters her ropes against the masts. The ship's bell clangs on the hour and half hour, and the bosun's whistle ever pierces the air with its piped orders. With all the din of London, I thought it could never be so noisy on a ship. But it is.

I've chickens for neighbours, and pigs, and a goat. They snort and cluck and bleat day and night, in pens on deck. I'm glad of their company and wish I might go near them more often. I've had milk out of the goat, straight from her teat. John Ramsey says she's aboard for the Gentlemen and Officers, so they might have fresh cream when they please.

Today, the 19th, Captain Cook gathered the Ship's Company on deck and read the Articles of War aloud. Captain is a clean-shaven man, strict and stern, with cold eyes. The Articles he read stated there would be no swearing of oaths, on board, no drunkenness, nor uncleanness. Good thing Captain hasn't had a whiff of me. The Articles declare cowardice, mutiny, and desertion to be punishable acts. They say naught of stowaways, but Francis Haite, John Ramsey, and Samuel Evans each glanced my way during Captain's reading.

Sunday 21st {Plymouth}

We toss at anchor. My stomach heaves and cramps and heaves again. And I'm bruised from head to toe.

I half wish Father would come aboard and take me home. I'm tired of being wet and hungry. Father knows by my letter that I've run out on the Butcher. But I did not write where I meant to go, nor what I meant to do, for when I sent the letter, I hardly knew my plans myself. Even if he knew, he would not come. I am a disappointment to Father. All my brothers are scholars. Only I could not settle to my studies. Father has no use for a son who will not learn his Latin.

Friday 26th {Off the Coast of England}

Samuel Evans, who has the largest hands I have ever seen, larger even than the Butcher's, found me at my journal, which has suffered from the damp despite its wrappings. He cannot read nor write and thinks it wondrous that a boy of eleven can do what a grown man cannot. "I could teach you," I told him. "when I am out of hiding." He laughed and nodded his large head. "Time does sit heavy on a seaman some days. It'd be a blessing to read away the hours."

Wednesday 31st to Thursday 1st September
{Lat 44°56' N, Long.9°9' W}

All day the sea rose, breaking over the deck. Captain had the men everywhere in the rigging, trying to save the ship from being torn to pieces by the wind.

Just before first watch the Bosun staggered to the side and shook his fist at the sea, cursing it for stealing his **skiff**. But ship's cook, Mr. Thompson, was angrier still. A dozen of his hens drowned in the storm. Mr. Thompson kept muttering how he was never to feed the entire Company if the sea kept killing his livestock. I'd never seen ship's cook so close before. He has but one hand!

skiff: a small light sailing ship

The storm, at last, is blown out and Endeavour floats in the sea again. The servant boy, John Charlton, comes past when he can, leaving bits to eat. He also brings with him good cheer with that kind face of his and that beaming smile. I don't know much about him but that he is from London, has a friendly nature, and at fifteen years of age has spent his last three years at sea. He says my red hair reminds him of his mother. He knows his way about, John Charlton does, and he knows the men who brought me abroad. They can be trusted, he said. They're good men.

The men at night sing songs of Spain, and John Charlton says soon we are passing there. He brought me the latitude and longitude readings so I might enter them in my journal and has promised to do so whenever he can. I asked John what I should do about coming out.

"Stay hidden," he said. "If you are discovered now," he said, "Captain may yet put you off on land and see you returned to England."

Friday 2nd {Between Cape Finisterre and Cape Ortegal}

Spain! I cannot see it from my hiding place, but I heard the cry. The Gentlemen brought their casting nets out and fetched in such creatures I can only imagine. Great were there exclamations of wonder. Their excitement makes my hiding so much more difficult to bear. That and the dampness of it all.

Saturday 3rd {Off the Coast of Spain}

Saw little of the Gentlemen on deck today. At times they are careless and leave a morsel, spiced meat or cheese. Mr. Parkinson, one of the artists Mr. Banks brought aboard to draw the plants and animals we shall see on this voyage, is particularly forgetful with his food. He is a young man with woman's hands. I am always interested to hear his observations. I have seen much in my imagination, listening to Mr. Parkinson's reflections.

Monday 5th

Mr. Banks received a bird from one of the sailors this morning. It had been tangled in the rigging. The bird died in Mr. Banks's hands. He had one of his servants rush it to Mr. Parkinson to be drawn. I like all animals, but birds are my favourites. The year after Mother died, when I lived with Grandmother, I would climb trees and watch the birds in their nests. I learned to imitate their calls, so they would come almost to my hand.

Mr. Banks has two greyhound dogs. They sniff at my hiding place in the shelter of the Pinnace. Ordinarily the sight of them would gladden me, but I fear the bad turn they could do me now if they should give me away. But with the pens of livestock around me, no one questions their excitement. Must be the pigs making them act so, Mr. Banks says.

Saturday 10th {Off the Coast, North Atlantic}

In the night I dreamed of the Butcher and woke with a start. My back burned, remembering the bite of his whip. Silently, I slipped out of the Pinnace and crept over to Goat. She nodded, looked me over with a single golden eye, and leaned her weight comfortingly against me.

Wednesday 14th {Isle of Madeira}

A terrible accident today. Captain moved *Endeavour* to a new berth this morning. The anchor did not hold fast on the first attempt and required to be sent again. It was brought up and **hove** out, but this time Mr. Weir, the Quartermaster, found his leg entangled in the anchor rope. In a heartbeat Mr. Weir was over the side along with the anchor. It was a desperate work to bring him back up. The men hove up the line with the greatest urgency. But despite their efforts they were too late. Mr. Weir was drowned.

hove: past tense of heave

How did the author make you feel you were experiencing life on board the Endeavour? *What sources do you think she used to find out information about Captain Cook and this voyage?*

Source: Karen Hesse, *Stowaway.* New York: Margaret K. McElderry Books, 2000.

Marie Antoinette, Princess of Versailles

by Kathryn Lasky

Marie Antoinette was the Austrian archduchess who became Queen of France in 1774. While her husband, King Louis XVI, was timid, she proved to be strong and decisive. Unfortunately, she was also frivolous and extravagant, a quality which angered her subjects. She and her husband ruled France during the period known as the French Revolution, which lasted from 1789 until 1799. The hatred of the French people for the queen contributed to the rebellion that overthrew the monarchy on August 10, 1792. Louis XVI was executed in January 1792, and Marie Antoinette was beheaded on October 14, 1793. Yet, the Queen who was so hated by her French subjects spent her childhood in the Hapsburg Palace in Vienna, Austria, where she was carefully prepared for her future role. Her youthful energy is evident in these fictional entries from her diary, written in the year before her marriage. As you read this selection, think about the life that the young girl was being trained for. What are Marie Antoinette's thoughts about becoming Queen of France?

January 1, 1769
Holfburg Palace, Vienna, Austria
I do solemnly promise to write in this diary given to me by my tutor, Abbé de Vermond, if not every day, at least every week, even though writing is not easy for me. For I shape my letters poorly and do not too often know the proper spelling. Still, this is my resolution for the new year.
Yours truly,
Archduchess Maria Antonia Josepha Johanna, daughter of Maria Theresa of Hapsburg, Empress of the Holy Roman Empire of the Germanic Nations, and the late Emperor Francis of Lorraine

January 3, 1769
My second time writing. I am keeping the resolution. Abbé de Vermond would be proud. I spelled the word *solemnly* correctly, too, I think. I am grateful to the Abbé for giving me this beautiful little diary. It is blue, the color of the sky, and has gold *fleurs de lis* engraved—the symbol of the French Court—or one of the many symbols. I must learn French! Here now I shall list all the things I must learn over the next year:
- to write and read French (I speak it well, as it is the language of the Court here)
- to dance in the French manner
- to walk in the manner of the French Court, as if I float in the immense panniers, or side hoops, of the French ladies' dresses
- to read better
- to write better

Why must I learn these things better than other girls my age, better than any of my brothers and sisters, of which I have fifteen? Why? Because I am to be Queen of France.

January 4, 1769
I now am refreshed so I shall explain. I am just thirteen and before I become Queen, I must first be what the French call the *Dauphine*. It is their word for the highest Princess in the land. The Dauphine is the wife of the Dauphin, the eldest son of the King. The French King is Louis XV. His son died. So now his eldest grandson is the Dauphin. His name is Louis Auguste. I am to marry him, probably next year. And when Louis XV dies, the Dauphin shall become King Louis XVI and I shall become Queen Marie Antoinette. Together we shall rule. But for now I am an Archduchess. I am thirteen and everyone calls me Antonia. I am not yet ready to be a Dauphine, let alone a Queen. Everyone tells me this at least sixteen times a day.

I am not ready because I do not write or read in my own language well, not to mention French. Although I am a better reader than writer, I just hate to read. But I am not stupid.
I think some thought I was stupid. But Abbé de Vermond told Mama that I am "clever" and that I am "capable of learning and eager to please" but that I am a bit lazy. He gave me this diary because he thought that if I had some place private to put my innermost thoughts, I would be more eager to write and thus improve my awful handwriting and spelling. He promises never to read it and, best of all, never to tell Mama I am keeping it. That is important because Mama is very nosy. Extremely nosy. I spelled that word, *extremely*, right. The Abbé would be very pleased but he shall never see it, if he keeps his promise. And I shall keep mine to him to keep writing. It does become easier each day. I think soon I shall write some more about my innermost thoughts. I'll make a list of the topics now for next time so I won't forget.
- Nosy Mama
- Caroline, my dearest sister
- My fat dead awful sister-in-law
- My favorite niece

January 5, 1769
This is fun. And Abbé de Vermond says I am improving in my writing and my reading. Already! And it has been only five days. Now to my list.
1) Nosy Mama—I love the Empress my mother very much. But she and I are quite different. She is not so lazy as me. She never wastes a minute. Indeed, when she was in labor giving birth to me she called a dentist to come along with the midwife, for she decided to have an old

rotten tooth pulled at the same time. She felt it was **efficient** to be in pain all at one time for two things. She is very orderly. Nothing is ever out of place. I misplace my handkerchief all the time and I lost my fan, the good one, that belonged to Brandy, my old governess whom Lulu replaced. Mama never forgets or misplaces things. But Mama is nosy. She wants to know everything I am doing, every bit I am learning. She tries to peek when I am getting dressed or undressed. She worries that my bosom might remain too flat, but with Caroline I remember her worrying that her bosom might be too large. "A heavy bosom adds age to a young girl." That is one of Mama's sayings. She has many sayings, including the family motto, which she recites all the time. "Others make war, but thou, oh happy Austria, make marriages." These words are written in Latin on many crests and emblems around the palace. But that is not enough for Mama. She says it all the time—in Latin, in French, in German, and in Italian.

efficient: productive without waste

Mama's goal is to marry all of us children off to Kings or Queens, Princes or Princesses, Dukes or Duchesses. That is how the Empire grows, gets new land, and friends or allies to help us in times of war. Through marriage we can perhaps get peace. It is a very good bargain, in Mama's mind.

I think that is why Mama is so nosy. To make marriages, she must stick her nose into all of our businesses. So far she has done well. My sister Maria Christina married Albert of Saxony, and he is now governor of the Austrian Netherlands, the part we call Hungary. Maria Amalia married the Duke of Parma and is therefore a Duchess in Italy. My brother Joseph married fat Josepha of Bavaria, and my favorite sister Caroline was wed to Ferdinand, King of Naples.

Marie Antoinette's marriage to the Dauphin of France was arranged by her mother for political purposes. She and her future husband had never even met when they became engaged. This was a common practice in European countries that were ruled by monarchies. Although her mother considered the match "a very good bargain," the marriage resulted in her daughter's death at the age of thirty-eight.

Source: Kathryn Lasky, *Marie Antoinette, Princess of Versailles*. New York: Scholastic Press, 2000.

Letter from Jamaica

by Simón Bolívar, 1815

In the early 1800s Spain still ruled most of Latin America and many people were poor or enslaved. After the revolution in Haiti, which was described in the document on page 133, the desire for independence swept across the region. Simón Bolívar (1783–1830), who as a boy had learned about the ideas of freedom around the world, rallied Latin Americans to fight for independence from Spain. At first Bolívar's efforts were unsuccessful, and he was forced to retreat to the island of Jamaica in 1815. While there, he wrote the following letter to an English friend, in which he predicted that South America would succeed in winning its independence. What do you think Bolívar meant by destiny?

September 6, 1815

Success will crown our efforts, because the destiny of America has been **irrevocably** decided; the tie that bound her to Spain has been **severed**. Only a **concept** maintained that tie and kept the parts of that immense monarchy together. That which formerly bound them now divides them. The hatred that the peninsula [of Spain] has inspired in us is greater than the ocean between us. It would be easier to have the two continents meet than to **reconcile** the spirits of the two countries. The habit of obedience; a community of interest, of understanding, of religion; mutual goodwill; a tender regard for the birthplace and good name of our forefathers; in short, all that gave rise to our hopes, came to us from Spain. . . . At present the **contrary** attitude persists: we are threatened with the fear of death, dishonor, and every harm; there is nothing we have not suffered at the hands of that unnatural step-mother—Spain. The veil has been torn **asunder**. We have already seen the light, and it is not our desire to be thrust back into darkness. The chains have been broken; we have been freed, and now our enemies seek to

irrevocably: impossible to change
severed: broken
concept: idea

reconcile: bring together

contrary: opposite

asunder: apart

enslave us anew. For this reason America fights desperately, and seldom has desperation failed to achieve victory. . . .

With respect to heroic and **hapless** Venezuela, events there have moved so rapidly and the **devastation** has been such that. . . [a] few women, children, and old men are all that remain. Most of the men have perished rather than be slaves; those who survive continue to fight furiously on the fields and in the inland towns, until they **expire** or hurl into the sea those who, **insatiable** in their thirst for blood and crimes, rival those first monsters who wiped out America's. . .[earliest people]. . . .

16,000,000 Americans either defend their rights or suffer **repression** at the hands of Spain, which although once the world's greatest empire, is now too weak, with what little is left her, to rule the new hemisphere or even to maintain herself in the old. . . . What madness for our enemy to hope to reconquer America when she has no navy, no funds, and almost no soldiers! . . .

Americans today, and perhaps to a greater extent than ever before, who live within the Spanish system occupy a position in society no better than that of serfs destined for labor, or at best they have no more status than that of mere consumers. . . . In short, do you wish to know what our future held?— simply the cultivation of the fields of indigo, grain, coffee, sugar cane, cacao, and cotton; cattle raising on the broad plains; hunting wild game in the jungles; digging in the earth to mine its gold— but even these limitations could never satisfy the greed of Spain.

So negative was our existence that I can find nothing comparable in any other civilized society, examine as I may the entire history of time and the politics of all nations. Is it not an outrage and a violation of human rights to expect a land so splendidly **endowed**, so vast, rich, and populous, to remain merely passive?. . .

More than anyone, I desire to see America **fashioned** into the greatest nation in the world, greatest not so much by virtue of her area and wealth as by her freedom and glory. . . .

From the **foregoing**, we can draw these conclusions: The American provinces are fighting for their freedom, and they will ultimately succeed.

hapless: unlucky
devastation: ruin

expire: die
insatiable: unable to be satisfied

repression: mistreatment

endowed: plentiful in resources

fashioned: shaped

foregoing: points stated before

After returning to South America, Bolívar led his troops on a difficult march across the steep, snow-covered Andes Mountains. His forces surprised the Spanish army in Colombia and defeated them in a battle that was the turning point in the struggle for independence. By 1824, with Bolívar's help, the Spanish colonies in South America had broken free from the Spanish empire. For his bold and heroic actions, South Americans remember Simón Bolívar as "The Liberator."

Source: Harold A. Bierck, Jr., ed., *Selected Writings of Bolívar.* New York: The Colonial Press, Inc., 1951.

WORKING IN THE MINES

by Ann Eggley and Elizabeth Eggley, 1842

One of the results of the Industrial Revolution, which began in England in the 1700s, was the use of child labor. Children as young as six often worked more than 12 hours a day in crowded mines and factories. In 1842 the British government began an investigation into the effects of child labor. Among the workers interviewed were two teenage sisters, Ann and Elizabeth Eggley. They both worked in the coal mines as "hurriers," people who pushed carts loaded with coal ore that weighed hundreds of pounds. As you read excerpts from their testimony to government officials, notice how the Eggleys feel about their work. Why do you think some people wanted to outlaw child labor?

Ann Eggley, 18 years old

We go [to work] at four in the morning, and sometimes at half-past four. We begin to work as soon as we get down. We get out after four, sometimes at five, in the evening. We work the whole time except an hour for dinner, and sometimes we haven't time to eat. I **hurry** by myself, and have done so for [a long time]. I know the **corves** are very very heavy. They are the biggest corves anywhere about. The work is far too hard for me; the sweat runs off me all over sometimes. I am very tired at night. Sometimes when we get home at night we have not power to wash us, and then we go to bed. Sometimes we fall asleep in the chair. Father said last night it was both a shame and a disgrace for girls to work as we do, but there was **nought** else for us to do. I have

hurry: push carts loaded with coal

corves: carts used in the mines

nought: nothing

93

tried to get **winding** to do, but could not. I begun to hurry when I was seven and I have been hurrying ever since. I have been 11 years in the pit. The girls are always tired. I was **poorly** twice this winter; it was with headache. I hurry for Robert Wiggins; he is not **akin** to me. I **riddle** for him. We all riddle . . . except the littlest. . . . We don't always get enough to eat and drink, but we get a good supper. I have known my father [to] go at two in the morning to work . . . and he didn't come out till four [in the afternoon]. I am quite sure that we work constantly 12 hours except on Saturdays. We wear trousers and our **shifts** in the pit, and great big shoes. . . . I never went to a dayschool. . . . I walk about and get the fresh air on Sundays. I have not learnt to read.

winding: raising coal to the surface of the mine

poorly: ill

akin: related

riddle: separate materials

shifts: loose shirts or dresses

Elizabeth Eggley, 16 years old

I am sister to the last witness. I hurry in the same pit, and work for my father. I find my work very much too hard for me. I hurry alone. It tires me in my arms and back most. We go to work between four and five in the morning. If we are not there by half past five we are not allowed to go down at all. We come out at four, five, or six at night as it happens. We stop in generally 12 hours, and sometimes longer. . . . I am sure it is very hard work and [it] tires us very much; it is too hard for girls to do. We sometimes go to sleep before we get to bed. We haven't a very good house; we have but two rooms for all the family. I have never been to school except four times. . . . I cannot read. . . .

The testimony of the Eggley sisters and other young workers made people in England more aware of the horrors of child labor. As a result of their testimony, Parliament passed new laws forbidding the employment of children under the age of 10 in the mines. Child labor, however, such as that described by the Eggleys, continued to exist in England for many more years.

Source: Erna Olafson Hellerstein, Leslie Parker Hume, and Karen M. Offen, eds., *Victorian Women*. Stanford, CA: Stanford University Press, 1981.

PROGRESS IN INDUSTRY

Advertisement, 1887

The Industrial Revolution began in England in the 1700s. Advancements in technology and manufacturing during this period made great changes in people's lives. The advertisement on this page is for a company that sold products that were developed during the Industrial Revolution. The locomotive was one of the great technological advances of this time. The first successful locomotive in the United States pulled its first train of cars on the South Carolina Railroad in December 1830. About a decade later the telegraph was invented by Samuel Morse (1791–1872). Many people were doubtful about the speed and usefulness of Morse's new invention. However, when the first telegraph message was sent from Washington, D.C., to Baltimore in May 1844 with news of the vice presidential nomination, everyone was impressed. The telegraph message arrived one and one-half hours ahead of the train that also carried the news! How does the advertisement below reflect the progress and excitement of the Industrial Revolution?

By 1900 the Industrial Revolution had spread to many countries throughout the world. How did the revolution change the way people traveled and the way they communicated? How would the world be different today if there had been no Industrial Revolution?

Source: Henry V. Poor, *Manual of the Railroads of the United States for 1887.* New York: Poor's Railroad Manual Co., 1887.

CLARA'S DIARY

by Clara Whitney, 1875–1887

Beginning about 1630, Japan chose to have very little contact with other nations. The borders began to open again in the 1850s, and by the early 1870s, many Japanese students came to the United States to attend college and gain skills they could take back to their country. During this period, called the "Meiji Restoration," there was a rise in industry in Japan that would forever change the country. In 1875 a 15-year-old American girl named Clara Whitney moved from Newark, New Jersey to Tokyo, Japan, where her father, William Whitney, planned to open a national business college. The following excerpts are from Clara's diary, which she kept throughout her life. What cultural traditions did Clara witness? What signs of cultural changes did she record?

Sunday, February 6, 1876:...After walking a short time we came to the [Shinto] temple which was not a large one, however. Several brass bells, shaped like large sleigh bells but having long ropes attached to them, hung around the porch.

This was the manner of worship. At a stand nearby the worshipers bought rice cakes wrapped up in little papers, further on they bought beans, and at the temple gate was a large tank of water for washing the hands and face before entering into the presence of the god. After washing they go up to the bells (if they can get to them) and pull long and well to attract the attention of the god. If they cannot reach the bells, they stand a ways off and throw beans and rice cakes in papers— the former are thrown into the temple or shrine, and the latter lodged on the roof. The people then clap their hands and bow their heads as they pray....

Friday, November 3, 1876: Today is His Majesty's birthday....How gay the streets were! Flags of all descriptions floated gaily from every window and door. Large flags, small flags, middle-sized flags, good flags, bad ones, and any kind of rag with a red spot on it were taken by our enthusiastic friends—the Japanese. Some of these emblems were evidently homemade. How they bristled out from every **casement**! What long avenues of "Rising Suns" [flags] we passed! At home we were not behind in style by any means, for we had two tall flags on our upper **verandah** guarding our homemade American **signal**. Mama said that as the sun in the center of the Japanese flag looks so much like the full moon, our stars harmonize very well with it....

casement: window

verandah: porch
signal: flag

Thursday, August 23, 1877: We went to the National Exhibition this afternoon and, though not as large as we expected, it was still a very fine affair. We went rather late, so that we had very little time to see all the sights. The Art Gallery was perfectly fascinating to me and appeared to be most attractive to the Japanese also, for it was full of people, some of whom in their flowing dresses and spread-out fans looked like statues themselves. It was with difficulty that I tore myself away from all the loveliness. We entered the Eastern Hall and found ourselves in the midst of cotton, canned fruit and other uninteresting things—although there was a nice bedroom set there. In the Machinery Hall we saw a loom invented by a Japanese. The Horticultural Hall was made up of dwarf pine trees and other botanical monstrosities. In the Agricultural Hall were very interesting collections of seeds and fruits from different provinces. The zoological section was not interesting because of the fierce-looking cows and horses there. But next to the Art Gallery, the Western Hall was the best, for in this were fine china, lacquered work, enameled ware, inlaid furniture and thousands of other pretty things.

Monday, March 25, 1878:...It is the day of the opening of the Central Telegraph Company and the building opposite us is decked with flags, lanterns, and evergreen arches, making a very pretty show.... There was a display of acrobatic feats by the firemen in front of the building. They came rushing over the bridge, shouting and bearing aloft the fireman's signal—a big banner of silver paper. Six men in succession ascended a ladder and performed marvelous feats of acrobatic skill. One man fell off, bumped his nose, and fainted.

Saturday, April 25, 1884: Today I met the Emperor of Japan. His Majesty sent invitations to the **legations** and to members of the Japanese aristocracy to come and visit him at the **Hamagoten** to see the cherry blossoms and to take lunch with him.... At last,... we were called to the space near the lake once more and bidden to form ourselves into a line, as His Majesty and the Empress were on their way.... The brilliant imperial procession then approached. At its head walked the Emperor in French military uniform.... He shook hands with the ministers and their ladies, bowed gracefully and smiled as he was made to understand their polite speeches through an interpreter.... The Empress came next in beautiful **brocade** robes, the outer one of deep lovely blue and brocaded with many rich designs.... Her Majesty also shook hands and made some pleasant remarks in reply to the polite speeches of the ministers.... It was a striking picture....

legations: foreign diplomats
Hamagoten: palace

brocade: heavy fabric with raised designs

In 1886 Clara Whitney married Kaji Umetaro, the son of a family friend, and a native of Japan. They had six children. Clara returned to live in the United States in 1900.

Source: Clara A.N. Whitney, *Clara's Diary: An American Girl in Meiji Japan*. Tokyo: Kodansha International, Ltd., 1978.

A STORMY CENTURY

*We fought injustice wherever
we found it, no matter how
large, or how small, and we
fought injustice to preserve
our own humanity.*

Nelson Mandela, 1994

ALL QUIET ON THE WESTERN FRONT

by Erich Maria Remarque, 1929

World War I was the first major conflict of the 20th century. From 1914 to 1918, millions of soldiers engaged in a new style of fighting called trench warfare. Rather than face each other on large battlefields, soldiers on both sides dug trenches, or deep ditches. From these trenches, soldiers fired guns and threw hand grenades in hopes of driving out the enemy. Trench warfare led to many deaths but few victories. In 1929 a former German soldier named Erich Maria Remarque (1898-1970) wrote a novel describing his experiences in World War I. As you read the following excerpt from All Quiet on the Western Front, *notice how Remarque re-creates the experience of trench warfare. How do you think the narrator feels about war?*

Quiet, I squat in a **shell-hole** and try to locate myself. More than once it has happened that some fellow has jumped joyfully into a trench, only then to discover that it was the wrong one.

shell-hole: crater formed by an exploded bomb

After a little time I listen again, but still I am not sure. The confusion of shell-holes now seems so **bewildering** that I can no longer tell in my **agitation** which way I should go. Perhaps I am crawling parallel to the lines, and that might go on forever. So I crawl round once again in a wide curve.

bewildering: confusing
agitation: nervousness

These [awful] rockets! They seem to burn for an hour, and a man cannot make the least movement without bringing the bullets whistling round.

But there is nothing for it, I must get out. **Falteringly** I work my way farther, I move off over the ground like a crab and rip my hands sorely on the jagged splinters, as sharp as razor blades. Often I think that the sky is becoming lighter on the horizon, but it may be merely my imagination. Then gradually I realize that to crawl in the right direction is a matter of life or death.

falteringly: unsteadily

A shell crashes. Almost immediately two others. And then it begins in earnest. A bombardment. Machine-guns rattle. Now there is nothing for it but to stay lying low. Apparently an attack is coming. Everywhere the rockets shoot up. **Unceasing.**

unceasing: unending

I lie huddled in a large shell-hole, my legs in the water up to the belly. When the attack starts I will let myself fall into the water, with my face as deep in the mud as I can keep it without suffocating. I must pretend to be dead.

Suddenly I hear the **barrage** lift. At once I slip down into the water, my helmet on the **nape** of my neck and my mouth just clear so that I can get a breath of air.

barrage: sound of exploding bombs

nape: back

I lie motionless;—somewhere something clanks, it stamps and stumbles nearer—all my nerves become taut and icy. It clatters over me and away, the first wave has passed. I have but this one shattering thought: What will you do if someone jumps into your shell-hole?— Swiftly I pull out my little dagger, grasp it fast and bury it in my hand once again under the mud. If anyone jumps in here I will go for him. It hammers in my forehead; at once, stab him clean through the throat, so that he cannot call out; that's the only way; he will be just as frightened as I am; when in terror we fall upon one another, then I must be first.

Now our **batteries** are firing. A shell lands near me. That makes me savage with fury, all it needs now is to be killed by our own shells; I curse and grind my teeth in the mud; it is a raving frenzy; in the end all I can do is groan and pray.

batteries: guns

The crash of the shells bursts in my ears. If our fellows make a counter-raid I will be saved. I press my head against the earth and listen to the muffled thunder, like the explosions of quarrying—and raise it again to listen for the sounds on top.

The machine-guns rattle. I know our barbed wire entanglements are strong and almost undamaged;—parts of them are charged with a powerful electric current. The rifle fire increases. They have not broken through; they have to retreat.

I sink down again, huddled, strained to the uttermost. The banging, the creeping, the clanging becomes audible. One single cry yelling amongst it all. They are raked with fire, the attack is **repulsed**.

repulsed: driven back

More than 8 million soldiers died in World War I. Many people called this conflict "the war to end all wars." But only 20 years after the end of World War I, an even more horrible war would break out in Europe. For a description of one part of this war, read The Art of Keeping Cool *on page 103.*

Source: Erich Maria Remarque, *All Quiet on the Western Front.* New York: Fawcett Crest, 1989.

Never Give Up the Fight

by Winston Churchill and Franklin Roosevelt, 1941

World War II began in Spetember 1939, when German forces invaded Poland. Soon after, the Germans conquered France, and they began bombing Britain. Britain and France were joined by Russia, which was invaded by Germany in the summer of 1941. They were known as the Allies. The United States supported the Allies but had not yet entered the war. Germany, Japan, and their forces were known as the Axis powers. The following are excerpts of speeches made during the war by two world leaders—British Prime Minister Winston Churchill and U.S. President Franklin Roosevelt.

Winston Churchill, October 29, 1941

Never give in, never give in, never, never, never—in nothing, great or small, large or **petty**—never give in except to **convictions** of honor and good sense. Never yield to force; never yield to the apparently overwhelming might of the enemy. We stood all alone a year ago, and to many countries it seemed that our account was closed, we were finished....

petty: minor
convictions: firm beliefs

Very different is the mood today. Britain, other nations thought, had drawn a sponge across her slate. But instead our country stood in the gap. There was no flinching and no thought of giving in; and by what seemed almost a miracle to those outside these Islands, though we ourselves never doubted it, we now find ourselves in a position where I say that we can be sure that we have only to persevere to conquer.

Franklin Roosevelt, December 8, 1941

Yesterday, December 7, 1941—a date which will live in **infamy**—the United States of America was suddenly and deliberately attacked by naval and air forces of the Empire of Japan....

infamy: memory of a wrongdoing

I believe that I interpret the will of the Congress and of the people when I assert that we will not only defend ourselves to the uttermost but will make it very certain that this form of **treachery** shall never again endanger us.

treachery: betrayal

Hostilities exist. There is no blinking at the fact that our people, our territory, and our interests are in grave danger.

With confidence in our armed forces—with the **unbounding** determination of our people—we will gain the **inevitable** triumph— so help us God.

unbounding: limitless
inevitable: certain

The United States entered the war in December 1941, after the Japanese attack on Pearl Harbor, Hawaii, that President Roosevelt refers to in the last excerpt above. The Allies ultimately defeated the Axis powers in August 1945. President Roosevelt did not live long enough to see the end of the war, however. He died in April 1945.

Sources: David Cannadine, ed., *Blood, Toil, Tears and Sweat: The Speeches of Winston Churchill*. Boston: Houghton Mifflin Company, 1989; John Bartlett, ed., *Familiar Quotations*. Boston: Little, Brown & Co., Fifteenth ed., 1980; B.D. Zevin, ed., *Nothing to Fear: The Selected Addresses of Franklin Delano Roosevelt, 1932-1945*. Boston: Houghton Mifflin Co., 1946.

The Art of Keeping Cool

by Janet Taylor Lisle

In February, 1942, during World War II, Robert moves with his mother and sister to his grandfather's home in Rhode Island. There he meets his cousin Elliot, an artist who prefers to keep his talent a secret. Unfortunately, in wartime no place in The Art of Keeping Cool is completely safe. While Nazi submarines torpedo U.S. ships off the coast, the townspeople are angered by the arrival of a German artist, Abel Hoffman, whom they believe is a spy. Despite their close friendship, Elliot and Robert react very differently to Hoffman's presence in their community. As you read this selection, consider how the dangers of wartime can arouse people's prejudices. Why do you think the two cousins feel so differently about the artist?

Without Elliot, I'd started playing baseball in the afternoons when my jobs around the house were done. A bunch of us were out hitting flies in the field beside the school when Abel came in to town for groceries and supplies one day about a week after he was arrested. He was taking dirty looks from almost everyone he passed. People were crossing the street to keep away from him. When Larry Bean from the filling station saw him heading for the post office, he yelled:

"Hey, it's the Nazi. Picking up your instructions, Nazi?"

We saw Abel look around and walk away fast. Then somebody, not one of us, threw a Coke bottle and it smashed to pieces on the street in front of him. He jumped like a spooked cat and ran up the steps to the post office, slamming the door after him. We all laughed. He looked so ridiculous.

While he was inside, Jerry Antler and Willie Vogel began to joke around about the way Abel talked. Willie was the kid whose dad had been killed in action, and he'd been getting kind of loud and **sassy** lately. He and Jerry had a little routine they'd worked up together after they'd overheard Abel in the post office one time. Abel was in there almost every week to pick up packages. He ordered painting supplies from somewhere and had them

sassy: vigorous, lively

103

shipped to him. A whole stream of stuff was always coming in from Boston or New York. No one could figure out where he got the money to buy it.

"Have-ensee post most wery please?" Willie would ask.

"What, not post?" Jerry would say. "Where what not post?"

Willie: "How where not post what?"

Jerry: "What not post commen where tomorrow, wery please?"

This would go on for a while, until everyone was practically on the ground laughing, which was how Abel found us when he came out that afternoon. He looked over and stared for a long second, then started away toward the grocery store.

I was laughing as hard as anyone, but when Abel stopped and stared that way, I quit and turned my back on him fast.

"What's the matter with you? You look like you saw a ghost," Jerry told me.

I didn't say anything, but five minutes later I got out there and went home. I thought Abel had seen me, had picked me out specially from everyone else there and given me a look. It made me wonder if the FBI agents had told him who talked, and I didn't want to be around when he came back down the road with his groceries.

Grandpa must have heard from one of his patients about the bottle-throwing incident because that night, he sounded off at the supper table.

"The fellow's a magnet for trouble. Arrest him on some charge, any charge, and get him out of here, that's what I say. By the time the FBI digs up enough evidence to prove anything, he'll have done whatever damage he's capable of, or it'll have been done to him."

"Now Harvey," Grandma said. "There's nothing to prove the poor man's doing anything wrong." She was still siding with her friend Agnes.

"He's doing wrong just by living here!" Grandpa said. "It's bad enough that he's one of those crackpot artists. Freeloaders, every one of them, Communists and kooks."

Across the table, I saw Elliot begin to chew on his hand. He was downstairs eating with us again, though he still didn't look well.

"On top of that, what's he think?" Grandpa went on. "That people around here aren't going to suspect a Kraut? We're at war with them, for pity's sake. Why is he here, on this coast, right next to our military installations? That's what I want to know. If he's what he says he is, why isn't he painting his rubbish in Kansas . . . or Ohio," Grandpa turned to look accusingly at me, "where he doesn't pose a risk? Anyone would think he was up to something. Maybe he is and maybe he isn't, but the man's asking for trouble. He's going to get it, too."

The dark twisted look that came over Elliot's face while he listened to this made me feel sick myself. I couldn't stand to see him hurt, even when I thought he was wrong. I saw how he hated Grandpa for the things he said, and at the same time, how he wouldn't allow himself to fight back, no matter what. I'd never known anyone like that and it really stumped me. If I could have stood up for Elliot, I would have. That night I almost did anyway. But Grandpa was right about Abel being a magnet for trouble. He was right about Abel asking for it by staying around.

After supper, I went up to Elliot's room, which I hadn't done for a while. He took this as a kind of peace sign and showed me a wild turkey egg he'd found. Wild turkey eggs were rare around Sachem's Head, as rare as wild turkeys themselves, so this was a real find.

"What are you going to do with your egg collection when you've found every egg there is? Sell it for a million dollars?" I asked him, kind of half-kidding.

"Well, first of all I'll never find every egg," he said.

"But what if you did?"

"I'd never sell it," Elliot said. "I'd never give it away to a museum or anything either. I'd just keep it and have it to go over whenever I wanted. Every single egg that's here, I know where I found it and how and when, so it's special. If I gave them away, no one would know anything about them. They'd just be this mass of old birds' eggs that people came to see because they were all together in one place. What good would that do?"

I don't know why, but I loved that answer. I looked at Elliot and just shook my head. It seemed to me that no one else in the world or in the history of the world would have thought that way about a dumb egg collection. Elliot was the only one.

A few minutes later, though, he brought the conversation around to a place I wish he wouldn't.

"I was at Abel's today," he said. "He's afraid to go into town, now."

"Well he should be afraid," I couldn't help saying.

"He doesn't dare go anywhere to paint, not even the beaches that are open," Elliot said. "He stays in the woods."

"Sounds like a smart idea. You know, if I were him, I might start thinking of other places to live."

Elliot shook his head. "He can't leave now. You should see what he's doing. Big oils, six feet across, that make it look like the sea is going to rise up and break through the surface."

Listening to Abel was like watching him paint.

"In old days, I have in Germany, many, many friends!" he bellowed. "We are young, poor, full with ideas!"

Then he whispered: "Where are they now, these talented ones? Hiding, like me. Arrested. Or worse, dead."

He leapt up suddenly and threw his arms in the air: "What to do! How to fight! Everywhere is evil now!"

He sat again, glaring into space while he made the next sentence in his mind.

In this way, we learned how, long before the war, he left his family's home in Berlin to go to an art school in the city of Frankfurt. There he met other young artists experimenting in ways he had never imagined possible. No longer was it good enough to draw, line by line, the simple appearance of things. Now one must learn to paint the invisible: hidden feelings and memories, terrors and passions, the submerged continents everyone knows are there but cannot speak about.

He began his own experiments.

"I wanted my paintings to roar!" he shouted to us. "To roar and . . . and . . . what is that called in the ocean? He asked Elliot, nodding toward the naval practice runs.

"Explosions? To explode?

"Yah, to explode. To make a big sound. But also to make silence. And quiet, like water dripping after a storm. A painting can do many things. It can make the eye hear."

In Germany, his work began to be noticed. **Expressionist**, it was called. He used paint straight from the tube. Pure colors. A tube of paint is like a stick of dynamite, he said. The surface of things is exploded. Inner landscapes are revealed.

Younger painters came and lived near him. He gained a reputation, supported himself comfortably, though he was never rich. He lived in city apartments, moved about to Munich, to Dresden, to Paris for a year, then home to Frankfurt, where he was appointed to a professor's post at the famous Art Academy.

But a new political order was growing in Germany. The Nazi Party came to power in 1933. Hitler and his circle dislike the new art. It looked crazy they said, as if mental patients had painted it. Good art does not try to confuse people or disgust them. It is clear and vigorous, straightforward and beautiful, and provides the public with uplifting subjects, natural landscapes and scenes of normal life.

Well, all right. Everyone is entitled to his or her own opinion. There is room for all kinds of art, all kinds of opinions in the world.

Except with Hitler, there was to be only one room, Abel Hoffman told us. Very soon, he and his brutish regime began to eliminate the other rooms. How? This is how.

A letter arrives from the new chairman of the art department. You are dismissed from your professorship at the Art Academy. The money for your post has been cut off. You must leave immediately, after ten years! Why? You have been judged an unfit artist, one of the degenerates who are trying to fool people, or corrupt them. When you go to interview for another teaching job, you are turned away. Your name is on a list. No one will hire you.

You find work painting wall decorations in office buildings. It's **demeaning** and physically exhausting, but helps pay the bills. You work on your own art, too, but sell less and less.

demeaning: degrading

One night, a knock comes on the door. It's the police, Hitler's dreaded Gestapo, accompanied by your landlord, wringing his hands.

—Are you Hoffman?

—Yes.

—You must leave at once. This apartment is needed by the state.

—But where can I go?

—That's your problem. What is this trash on the floor, your paintings?

—Yes.

—We must **confiscate** them.

confiscate: to seize by or as if by authority

—Why?

—We're under orders.

—But, where will you take them?

—We'll let you know.

The paintings, your newest and best, are carried away. They disappear. No one will tell you where they are. You move in with a friend. Before long, you're fired from your wall painting job. Why? You're one of those **blacklisted** artists. Your employer has a business to protect. You are too risky.

blacklisted: those who are disapproved of or are to be punished or boycotted

You are officially notified that your work has been declared "obscene" and anti-German in spirit. The government has ordered it removed from museums and public places. It cannot be sold. Dealers will be prosecuted. "But I paint nature!" you cry. "You have deformed nature," comes the reply.

One night in the town square, a huge bonfire is lit for the enjoyment of the people. The fuel is books, furniture, musical manuscripts, Parisian hats, paintings, photographs, and masses of indistinguishable junk. In the fire, the painter catches sight of a pile of his canvases just beginning to ignite. There's the one he painted in Dresden, of the bridge and the birds feeding below in the snow. He never wanted to sell it because it reminded him of himself that winter. Solitary, cold, his young followers pecking for crumbs nearby.

The painter hurls himself toward the fire. He tries to rescue his work but is dragged back by several people in the crowd. Is he crazy? Does he want to kill himself? He stares at the flames in shock. The paint on his painting begins to melt and char. He turns away in tears, runs his hand through his hair. He can't bear to watch.

Do you think the townspeople were justified in treating Abel Hoffman the way they did? Can you think of anything he can do or say to defend himself? What do you think of the way he was treated by the Nazis?

Source: Janet Taylor Lisle. *The Art of Keeping Cool.* New York: Atheneum Books for Young Readers, 2000.

The War Years in Vietnam

by Le Ly Hayslip, 1989

Vietnam is a beautiful land of forests, rice fields, rivers, and mountains. Long, bitter wars, however, have scarred the land and the lives of its people during much of this century. The longest conflict, between North Vietnam and South Vietnam, lasted from the 1950s until 1975. For many of those years, the United States fought in this war on the side of South Vietnam. Le Ly Hayslip was only 12 years old when American soldiers first entered her small village in Vietnam. Because opposing armies competed in the countryside for people's loyalties, Le Ly Hayslip found herself both tortured by the South Vietnamese and sentenced to death by the North Vietnamese. In the excerpt below from her book When Heaven and Earth Changed Places, *Le Ly Hayslip recalls her wartime experiences. What lessons do you think she learned from her father?*

Once, when I was the only child at home, my mother went to [the city of] Da Nang to visit Uncle Nhu, and my father had to take care of me. I woke up from my nap in the empty house and cried for my mother. My father came in from the yard and reassured me, but I was still cranky and continued crying. Finally, he gave me a rice cookie to shut me up. Needless to say, this was a tactic my mother never used.

The next afternoon I woke up and although I was not feeling cranky, I thought a rice cookie might be nice. I cried a fake cry and my father came running in.

"What's this?" he asked, making a worried face. "Little Bay Ly doesn't want a cookie?"

I was confused again.

"Look under your pillow," he said with a smile.

I twisted around and saw that, while I was sleeping, he had placed a rice cookie under my pillow. We both laughed and he picked me up like a sack of rice and carried me outside while I gobbled the cookie.

In the yard, he plunked me down under a tree and told me some stories. After that, he got some scraps of wood and showed me how to make things: a doorstep for my mother and a toy duck for me. . . . My father showed me the mystery of hammers and explained the customs of our people.

His knowledge of the Vietnamese went back to the Chinese Wars in ancient times. I learned how one of my distant ancestors, a woman named Phung Thi Chinh, led Vietnamese fighters against the **Han**. In one battle, even though she was pregnant and surrounded by Chinese, she delivered the baby, tied it to her back, and cut her way to safety wielding a sword in each hand. I was amazed at this warrior's bravery and impressed that I was her **descendant**. Even more, I was amazed and impressed by my father's pride in her accomplishments . . . and his belief that I was worthy of her example. . . .

Han: an ancient Chinese dynasty

descendant: relative

Never again did I cry after my nap. Phung Thi women were too strong for that. Besides, I was my father's daughter and we had many things to do together. . . .

The next day, I took some water out to him in the fields. My mother was due home any time and I used every opportunity to step outside and watch for her. My father stopped working, drank gratefully, then took my hand and led me to the top of a nearby hill. It had a good view of the village and the land beyond it, almost to the ocean. I thought he was going to show me my mother coming back, but he had something else in mind.

He said, "Bay Ly, you see all this here? This is the Vietnam we have been talking about. You understand that a country is more than a lot of dirt, rivers, and forests, don't you?"

I said, "Yes, I understand." After all, we had learned in school that one's country is as sacred as a father's grave.

"Good. You know, some of these lands are battlefields where your brothers and cousins are fighting. They may never come back. Even your sisters have all left home in search of a better life. You are the only one left in my house. If the enemy comes back, you must be both a daughter and a son. I told you how the Chinese used to rule our land. People in this village had to risk their lives diving in the ocean just to find pearls for the Chinese emperor's gown. They had to risk tigers and snakes in the jungle just to find herbs for his table. Their payment for this hardship was a bowl of rice and another day of life. That is why. . . Phung Thi Chinh fought so hard to expel the Chinese. When the French came, it was the same old story. Your mother and I were taken to Da Nang to build a runway for their airplanes. We labored from sunup to sundown and well after dark. . . . Our reward was a bowl of rice and another day of life. Freedom is never a gift, Bay Ly. It must be won and won again. Do you understand?"

I said that I did. . . .

"Hey." He poked me in the ribs. "Are you getting hungry for lunch?"

"No. I want to learn how to take care of the farm. What happens

109

if the soldiers come back? What did you and Mother do when the soldiers came?"

My father squatted on the dusty hilltop and wiped the sweat from his forehead. "The first thing I did was to tell myself that it was my duty to survive—to take care of my family and my farm. That is a tricky job in wartime. It's as hard as being a soldier. . . . You may remember the night I sent you and your brothers and sisters away with your mother to Da Nang."

"You didn't go with us!" My voice still held the horror of the night I thought I had lost my father.

"Right! I stayed near the village—right on this hill—to keep an eye on the enemy and on our house. If they really wanted to destroy the village, I would save some of our things so that we could start over. Sure enough, that was their plan.

"The real problem was to keep things safe and avoid being captured. Their patrols were everywhere. Sometimes I went so deep in the forest that I worried about getting lost, but all I had to do was follow the smoke from the burning huts and I could find my way back.

"Once, I was trapped between two patrols that had camped on both sides of a river. I had to wait in the water for two days before one of them moved on. When I got out, my skin was **shriveled** like an old melon. I was so cold I could hardly move. From the waist down, my body was black with **leeches**. But it was worth all the pain. When your mother came back, we still had some furniture and tools to cultivate the earth. Many people lost everything. Yes, we were very lucky."

shriveled: wrinkled

leeches: worms that suck blood

My father put his arms around me. "My brother Huong—your uncle Huong—had three sons and four daughters. Of his four daughters, only one is still alive. Of his three sons, two went north to **Hanoi** and one went south to **Saigon**. Huong's house is very empty.". . .

My father drew me out to arm's length and looked me squarely in the eye. "Now, Bay Ly, do you understand what your job is?"

I squared my shoulders and put on a soldier's face. "My job is to **avenge** my family. To protect my farm by killing the enemy. I must become a woman warrior like Phung Thi Chinh!"

Hanoi: the capital of North Vietnam at the time

Saigon: the capital of South Vietnam at the time

avenge: seek revenge for

My father laughed and pulled me close. "No, little peach blossom. Your job is to stay alive—to keep an eye on things and keep the village safe. . . . Most of all, it is to live in peace and tend the shrine of our **ancestors**. Do these things well, Bay Ly, and you will be worth more than any soldier who ever took up a sword."

ancestors: family members who lived long ago

Le Ly Hayslip survived the Vietnam War and fled to the United States with her children in 1970. Five years later the war finally ended with the victory of the North Vietnamese. Le Ly Hayslip returned to her homeland in 1986 and had a reunion with her mother and other family members. She now lives in California, where she founded the East Meets West Foundation, a charitable relief and world peace group.

Source: Le Ly Hayslip with Jay Wurts, *When Heaven and Earth Changed Places.* New York: Doubleday, 1989.

Gandhi

by Leonard Everett Fisher

In the early 1900s, many people in India began fighting to win their country's independence from Great Britain. The leader of this movement was a lawyer named Mohandas Gandhi (1869 - 1948). Before returning to his homeland Gandhi lived in South Africa for twenty-two years. There he succeeded in changing certain laws that discriminated against the rights of Indian people. In this excerpt from a biography of his life, the writer describes the struggle faced by Gandhi and his followers. What kind of person do you think he was? What people and events influenced Gandhi to protest injustice? How did his experience in South Africa prepare him for his future role as India's leader?

India, a vast subcontinent of South Asia, is one of the world's oldest civilizations. Indian culture dates back at least five thousand years.

In 1609, the mogul rulers gave valuable trading rights, for spices and cloth, to the British East India Company. England quickly established a commercial foothold in the country and sent troops to protect its interests. Now, with British soldiers planted on Indain soil, England imposed an often brutal rule over a people whose culture and traditions differed greatly from its own.

India whose population was at least ten and a half times greater than England's, on a land mass about one-third the size of what is now the United States, became an English colony. Its people were mostly Hindu, followers of the country's chief religion. Muslims formed a large minority group. Victims of terrible poverty and overcrowding, more than half of India's people, Hindu and Muslim alike, died from disease and starvation by the time they were thirty. Those who lived would serve tiny England, an island monarchy, for the next 200 years.

Seventy thousand people lived in ancient Porbandar, a small city on India's west coast, when Mohanda Karamchand Gandhi was born there on October 2, 1869. He was the youngest of six children.

His father, Karamchand, or "Kaba," Gandhi, was a Hindu and three times a widower. He was a skilled but underpaid diplomat and he struggled to make ends meet. Kaba Gandhi worked as a minister to the British for the Maharaja of Porbandar. The very wealthy **maharaja** ran the town, but only because the British let him. Kaba kept the British at bay and the maharaja on his throne. Mohandas's mother, Putlibai, was a devout Hindu who prayed and fasted continuously.

Kabu and Putlibai Gandhi, together with Kaba's five brothers, their wives, and numerous children and grandchildren, lived crowded together in a three-story house. When Mohandas was seven years old, Kaba moved his entire family east to Rajkot. As minister to the maharaja there, he was jailed by the British for defending the prince against British insults. His father's politics and his mother's religious beliefs were important influences on young Gandhi.

By the time Mohandas was thirteen years old, he was married off to Kasturbai Makanji, who was the same age. The two teenagers hardly knew each other. According to custom, their parents had arranged for the wedding. The marriage, however, lasted for sixty-two years, and through four sons. In 1944 Kasturbai died in a British prison in India. She had been jailed for protesting colonial rule.

At nineteen, Mohandas was shipped off to London, England, to attend law school. His family had scraped together all their money in the hope that Mohandas, as a British-educated lawyer, would bring them position and wealth.

Mohandas went home in 1891 with a British law degree. He began practicing in Bombay, the country's largest city, seventy-five miles south of Porbandar. But his only clients were too poor to pay him. His shyness was so intense that Mohandas could hardly talk in front of Bombay judges and juries. His family had spent its savings trying to make him a success, and Mohandas was turning into a failure.

An opportunity came in 1893. Gandhi was asked to represent an Indian company in a civil suit in South Africa, another British colony. Gandhi jumped at the chance. He left India for the city of Durban in the province of Natal, the center of Indian culture in South Africa. He was to be gone a year.

After working for several weeks in Durban, Gandhi bought a first-class seat on a train to Pretoria. That night he was kicked off the train for refusing to sit in the baggage car. The conductor said that "sammies"—an insulting South African term for the brown-skinned people of India—belonged in the baggage car. That was the law as set down by the white Englishmen and Boers who ran the country. The Boers were farmers, descendants of early Dutch settlers of the region.

Gandhi quickly learned that the Indian people were treated more unjustly in colonial South Africa than they were in colonial India. Gandhi arrived in Pretoria by stagecoach, after having been forced to sit outside the carriage on the coachman's footboard, next to the driver. Outraged by the experience, he resolved to fight back, legally. Overcoming his natural shyness, Gandhi sued the railroad that had denied him his rightful seat, and won a grudging victory. The law was changed so that all Indians could sit in the seat to which their tickets entitled them—provided they wore English-style clothing. Word of this victory spread quickly, and Gandhi soon became a champion of Indian rights in South Africa and, indirectly, a spokesman for all the powerless nonwhites there.

Between 1907 and 1914, Gandhi and his followers, the Satyagrahis—"insisters on truth and love"—were repeatedly jailed as they peacefully refused to submit to unjust laws. By 1914, more than one hundred thousand Indians were either in jail or on strike.

Annoyed with white bigotry, Gandhi returned to the plain, loose-fitting wraparound garments of his Hindu heritage. His clothing became both a symbol of his defiance of white culture and an image that brought him closer to his own people.

The whole world criticized the unyielding policies of the South African government, now headed by Jan Christian Smuts, the Boer general defeated by the British in the Boer War.

Wealthy sympathizers of the penniless and homeless Satyagrahis established a huge farm outside Johannesburg to care for them. It was called Tolstoy Farm after the famed Russian author who preached nonviolence. There, Gandhi learned the crafts of weaving, carpentry, and leather working.

In 1914, South Africa, bowing to world opinion, the outrage of Great Britain itself, and the untiring leadership of Mohandas K. Gandhi, was ready to give in. Gandhi threatened to bring the government to its knees, with a march of thousands, if the cruel laws against Indians were not abolished immediately. South Africa, already locked in a paralyzing railway strike, could withstand no more conflict and passed the Indian Relief Act, putting an end to most of those laws.

Gandhi had won a great victory for racial equality and civil rights. "Democracy," he wrote, "is the finest thing in the world. . . He [General Smuts] started with being my bitterest opponent. . . Today he is my warmest friend."

In 1915, following the outbreak of World War I (1914–1918), Gandhi returned to India. Not all Indians welcomed him home, however. His ability to organize the people, and his vision of sacrifice and nonviolent disobedience made wealthy maharajas, well-connected businessmen, and the British nervous.

During this wartime period, some people thought that India should help Britain in return for more favorable conditions. Others wanted to revolt while England was busy fighting Germany. Gandhi insisted that India help England win the war. He felt that India would be rewarded with self-rule for this service.

Half a million Indians answered the call and fought alongside the British during the war. Yet India was not rewarded. Disappointed, Gandhi encouraged a movement for independence. In 1919, Great Britain passed censorship laws, banned freedom of assembly, and Gandhi's own writings. Gandhi and his followers refused to obey. Thousands were jailed. He called for a national nonviolent strike.

"Nonviolence," he preached, "is a weapon for the brave."

Despite Gandhi's call for peaceful protest, violence did occur. Three Englishmen died in riots at Amritsar. In a separate incident, fifteen thousand unarmed Amritsaris held an illegal meeting to protest the loss of their civil liberties. The British army fired on the crowd. Four hundred died. More than one thousand were wounded. Gandhi, outraged by the British action, decided to end his loyalty to the crown.

In 1920, nearly fifteen thousand delegates to the Indian National Congress voted for independence by peaceful means,. Not all in India were comfortable with this position. Many upper-class Indians with British educations who owned property and had British pounds in their bank accounts saw their privileged futures at risk. But brushing aside these special interests, the great mass of Indians adopted Gandhi's ideas of satyagraha—truth and love—and refused to obey British colonial laws. Muslims and Hindus, who had previously fought against each other over religious differences, now joined together in loosening India from England.

Gandhi and his Muslim allies whipped up support for independence. Wherever Gandhi traveled, the common people fell at his feet, worshipping him as a divine messenger sent by God to free them. They began calling him mahatma ("Great Soul").

In 1921, fifty-two-year-old Mahatma Gandhi, now a weaver of homespun cloth began to wear nothing more than a poor man's loincloth, shawl, and sandals. With his simple manner, he stood as a symbol of India's anger over its colonial status. Gandhi's small body and tiny voice, no outward challenge to British power, were nevertheless recognized by millions of Indians as the **essence** of their nonviolent defiance of British authority.

essence: the real nature of something

114

Between 1922 and 1924 Gandhi was imprisoned for criticizing the British government. In 1930 he led a 241-mile march for salt, the poor family's staple, to protest the tax the British placed on it. Thousands of marchers were jailed. Nonviolent protests erupted nationwide. British police clubbed the protesters. No one struck back. "Nothing but organized nonviolence," wrote Gandhi, "can check the organized violence of the British government." Gandhi fasted to call the world's attention to India's plight.

With Britain occupied by World War II (1939-1945), Gandhi demanded independence. But, he said, "We do not seek our independence out of Britain's ruin." Described as a "half-naked **seditionist**" by a British official, Gandhi called for massive civil disobedience. He and many of his followers, including his wife, Kasturbai, were jailed for treason. With Gandhi imprisoned, there was no one to control the mob violence. The people rioted.

seditionist: a person who incites resistance against lawful authority

In 1946, a war-weary England proposed independence. But some Indian Muslims wanted their own country, and when the British left India on August 15, 1947, fighting, known as the Partition riots, broke out between the Muslims and the Hindus. Finally, Pakistan, a Muslim state, was carved out of West and East India. What remained of India in between would be Hindu.

Although the struggle for civil rights was far from over, Mahatma Gandhi's long fight for India's freedom had been won.

Gandhi's nonviolent campaign was a success, and in 1947 India won its independence from Great Britain. His belief in protesting injustice through nonviolent methods influenced leaders in other countries, including the great American civil rights leader, Dr. Martin Luther King, Jr.

Source. Leonard Everett Fisher, *Gandhi.* New York: Atheneum Books for Young Readers, 1995.

Road to Peace

by Yasir Arafat and Yitzhak Rabin, 1993 and 1995

The Israeli and Palestinian people have known a great deal of conflict since the nation of Israel was founded in Palestine in 1948. When Yitzhak Rabin (YIHTS hahk rah BEEN) (1922-1995) became prime minister in 1992, he pledged to work toward peace with the Palestinians. This led to secret meetings in Oslo, Norway, which were successful in achieving a peace agreement which was called the "Declaration of Principles." The first two speeches excerpted below were made at the White House on September 13, 1993, at the signing of the agreement. Yitzhak Rabin and Palestinian leader Yasir Arafat (YAH sur AHR uh fat) (b. 1929) received the 1994 Nobel Peace Prize for their work on the agreement. They signed a second agreement at the White House on September 28, 1995. What views do these leaders seem to have in common?

Speech by Yasir Arafat, September 1993

*I*n the name of God, the most merciful, the passionate, Mr. President, ladies and gentlemen, I would like to express our tremendous appreciation to President Clinton and to his administration for sponsoring this historic event which the entire world has been waiting for.

Mr. President, I am taking this opportunity to assure you and to assure the great American people that we share your values for freedom, justice and human rights…

My people are hoping that this agreement which we are signing today will **usher in** an age of peace, coexistence and equal rights. We are relying on your role, Mr. President, and on the role of all the countries which believe that without peace in the Middle East, peace in the world will not be complete….

usher in: bring about

Now as we stand on the **threshold** of this new historic era, let me address the people of Israel and their leaders, with whom we are meeting today for the first time, and let me assure them that the difficult decision we reached together was one that required great and exceptional courage.

threshold: entranceway

We will need more courage and **determination** to continue the course of building coexistence and peace between us. This is possible and it will happen with **mutual** determination and with the effort that will be made with all parties on all the tracks to establish the foundations of a just and comprehensive peace….

determination: firm purpose

mutual: shared

[P]utting an end to [the Palestinian's] feelings of being wronged and of having suffered an historic injustice is the strongest guarantee to achieve coexistence and openness between our two peoples and future generations. Our two peoples are awaiting today this historic hope, and they want to give peace a real chance….

I thank you, Mr. President. We hope that our meeting will be a new beginning for **fruitful** and effective relations between the American people and the Palestinian people....

fruitful: productive

Ladies and gentlemen, the battle for peace is the most difficult battle of our lives. It deserves our **utmost** efforts because the land of peace, the land of peace yearns for a just and comprehensive peace. Thank you.

utmost: greatest

Speech by Yitzhak Rabin, September 1993

President Clinton, the President of the United States, your excellencies, ladies and gentlemen. This signing of the Israeli-Palestinian declaration of principles here today is not so easy, neither for myself as a soldier in Israel's wars, nor for the people of Israel, nor for the Jewish people in the **Diaspora** who are watching us now with great hope mixed with **apprehension**. It is certainly not easy for the families of the victims of the wars, violence, terror, whose pain will never heal, for the many thousands who defended our lives with their own and have even sacrificed their lives for our own. For them, this ceremony has come too late.

Diaspora: the scattering of Jews to many parts of the world

apprehension: fear

Today, on the eve of an opportunity for peace, and perhaps an end to violence and wars, we remember each and every one of them with everlasting love. We have come from Jerusalem, the ancient and eternal capital of the Jewish people. We have come from an **anguished** and grieving land. We have come from a people, a home, a family that has not known a single year, not a single month, in which mothers have not wept for their sons. We have come to try and put an end to the hostilities so that our children, and our children's children, will no longer experience the painful cost of war, violence and terror. We have come to secure their lives and to ease the sorrow and the painful memories of the past, to hope and pray for peace.

anguished: suffering

Let me say to you, the Palestinians, we are **destined** to live together on the same soil in the same land. We, the soldiers who have returned from battles stained with blood; we who have seen our relatives and friends killed before our eyes; we who have attended their funerals and cannot look into the eyes of their parents; we who have come from a land where parents bury their children: we who have fought against you, the Palestinians, we say to you today in a loud and a clear voice, enough of blood and tears. Enough!...

destined: fated

Today here in Washington at the White House, we will begin a new **reckoning in** the relations between peoples, between parents tired of war, between children who will not know war.... Ladies and gentlemen, the time for peace has come...

reckoning in: evaluation of

In the Jewish tradition, it is customary to conclude our prayers with the word "Amen." With your permission, men of peace, I shall conclude with words taken from the prayer recited by Jews daily. I would ask the entire audience to join me in saying "Amen."

May He who makes peace on High, make peace for us and all Israel. Amen.

Speech by Yasir Arafat, September 1995

It has been two years since we met at the White House to sign the Declaration of Principles, to which we and our Israeli partners have agreed to in Oslo. We meet again today to make new headway in giving hope to this historic process...

Today, standing before you, I tell you with courage and a sense of responsibility that our participation in the great peace process means that we are betting everything on the future....

From this day on we do not want to see any waste of or threat to any innocent Palestinian life or any innocent Israeli life. Enough killing and enough killing of innocent people....

For us to succeed... we are bound to base the emerging Palestinian political system on the principles of liberty, democracy, separation of powers, freedom of expression, and national **initiative**. We are also bound to continue building Palestinian institutions and the Palestinian national economy.

initiative: right of citizens to rule themselves

But this enterprise is still in its early stages and our institutions have yet to mature. The road ahead remains long, indeed.

Speech by Yitzhak Rabin, September 1995

The sight you see—you see before you at this moment was impossible, was unthinkable just two years ago. Only poets dreamt of it. And to our great pain, soldier and civilians went to their death to make this moment possible. Here we stand before you, men who fate and history have sent on a mission of peace to end once and for all 100 years of bloodshed....

Ladies and gentlemen, this week the Jewish people in its thousands of places of **dispersion** has marked a new year, and in their Holy Day prayers, Jews everywhere are saying—May we—I'm translating it to the best of my capability.

dispersion: separation

May we be remembered and **inscribed** before you in the Book of Life and of blessing and peace and prosperity, of deliverance and comfort and opportunity, we and all who **people** the House of Israel, for a good life and peace. These are my wishes to all the Jewish people. These are my wishes to all the citizens of Israel: a good life and a peace. These are also our wishes to our neighbors, to all the world peoples: a good life and peace.

inscribed: written

people: populate

Yitzhak Rabin did not live to see his wish for peace realized. He fell victim to violence on November 4, 1995. Rabin was shot and killed at a peace rally in Tel Aviv by a young Israeli who opposed the peace agreements with the Palestinians. In the words of Yasir Arafat, "the road ahead remains long, indeed."

Sources: Yasir Arafat and Yitzhak Rabin, *Declaration of Principles on Interim Self-Government Arrangements*. Ministry of Foreign Affairs, Government of Israel, 1993; *New York Times*, Sept. 29, 1995.

U.S. ATTACKED

New York Times Headline

On September 11, 2001, America was changed forever. Terrorists hijacked three commercial planes and crashed them into the twin towers of the World Trade Center in the financial district of New York City, and the Pentagon building outside Washington, D.C.. A fourth hijacked plane crashed into a field near Pittsburgh after passengers fought back against the hijackers. About 3,000 people were killed in the attack, including hundreds of New York City firefighters, police officers, and other rescue workers. Most of the casualties died when the World Trade Center towers collapsed as a result of the explosions and fire caused by the impact of the airplanes. Most victims were Americans; however, people from more than 60 other nations also died in the attacks. How does this headline from the New York Times capture the horror of the tragedy?

September 14 was declared a day of national mourning and remembrance for the victims of the attacks. On September 15, President George W. Bush addressed the nation, telling Americans that "We're at war." Less than a month later, on October 7, the United States and Great Britain began air attacks against Afghanistan, where the terrorist leader Osama bin Laden, had planned the attacks against the United States.

THE VISION THAT I SEE

by Kwame Nkrumah

During the 1800s European nations divided Africa into colonies and ruled almost the entire continent. In the middle 1900s, however, many Africans began fighting to regain their independence and freedom and to bring an end to this practice, called colonialism. One leader of this fight was Jomo Kenyatta. Another major leader in the struggle against imperialism and colonial rule was Kwame Nkrumah (KWAHM ee en KROO muh, 1909–1972), a member of the Nzima people. Nkrumah was born in Nkroful, a village in the British colony called the Gold Coast. Although imprisoned for his beliefs, Nkrumah continued to fight for an end to colonialism. In this speech, delivered in the 1950s, Nkrumah expresses his hopes for the Gold Coast and the rest of Africa. As you read an excerpt from this speech, notice Nkrumah's goals and beliefs. How does Nkrumah use history to support his ideas?

The subject I have chosen to address you on this evening is "The Vision that I See." . . . It is better to be free to manage, or mismanage, your own affairs, than not to be free to mismanage or manage your own affairs. . . .

You know, **Providence** must be at work. I don't want to go back into history because I might be repeating sad memories but imagine the whole question of the slave trade, how Negroes from the West Coast of Africa were all carried over to the United States. And look into Negro history. You see the suffering and **tribulation** these people went through, and yet they survived in the United States of America and the **West Indies**. That's Providence. God Himself came, and, as in the days of Moses and the Israelites, who spent so many hard years in Egypt under all kinds of suffering, what was the result? The day came, yes, when God Himself brought up the man, and that man led them out of Egypt. A greater **exodus** is coming in Africa today, and that exodus will be established when there is a united, free and independent West Africa.

Again I don't want to bore you with history. It is a sad story. Look at the whole country of Africa today. With the possible exception of Liberia, Egypt and Ethiopia, the entire country is divided and subdivided. . . .

Africa for the Africans! Is this some new concept that has come into being? . . . no! We are bringing into being another Africa for Africans, with a different concept, and that concept is what? A free and independent state in Africa. We want to be able to govern ourselves

providence: God's guidance of human destiny

tribulation: pain

West Indies: Caribbean islands

exodus: mass departure

in this country of ours without outside interference. And we are going to see that it is done.

Ladies and gentlemen, a people without a Government of their own is silly and absurd. Let us therefore **forge ahead** and develop our own countries, politically and economically. We must work for a greater glory and majesty, greater than the civilizations of our **grandsires**, the civilization of Ghana, the civilization of the [Mali] Empire and the civilization of the [Songhai] Empire. Long before the slave trade, long before Imperialistic rivalries in Africa began, civilizations of the Ghana Empire were in existence. And here, you even discover that at one time, at the great University of Timbuktu, Africans **versed** in the science of art and learning were studying their works translated in Greek and Hebrew, and at the same time exchanging professors with the University of Cordova in Spain. These were the brains, and today they come and tell us that we cannot do it. No, give the African a chance and he will show you that he can do it. . . .

And not only that, there have been great Africans, . . . who have distinguished themselves in the **cabinet** and in the field of battle. I need mention only a few: Anthony Amu, a man from the **Gold Coast**, was the first African to graduate with the degree of doctor of philosophy from the University of Wittenberg. Amu became professor of philosophy at the University of Berlin, 1954. He was an African. He came and died in the Gold Coast. That was a brain. . . . And not only that. In the field of battle there is **Toussaint**. Yes, these are the men who have put up the torch of light that we men of today, the youth of Africa, want to learn and **emulate** them, forge ahead, until Africa is **redeemed**, until we are free to manage or mismanage our own affairs in this country.

We believe in the equality of races. We believe in the freedom of the people of all races. We believe in cooperation. In fact it has been one of my **theses** that in this struggle of ours, in this struggle to redeem Africa, we are fighting not against race and colour and creed. We are fighting against a system—a system which degrades and exploits, and wherever we find that system, that system must be **liquidated**. Yes, we believe in peace and cooperation among all countries, but we also **abhor** Colonialism and Imperialism. We abhor man's inhumanity against man. . . .

We must learn to live together. The age of **aristocracy** is gone. God made all of us equal. In the sight of God we are one. We must combine. . . .

forge ahead: move forward

grandsires: male ancestors

versed: educated

cabinet: government

Gold Coast: present-day country of Ghana

Toussaint: Toussaint L'Ouverture, the liberator of Haiti

emulate: equal or surpass

redeemed: freed

theses: beliefs

liquidated: destroyed

abhor: hate

aristocracy: government by a privileged upper class

Four years after delivering this speech, Kwame Nkrumah helped lead his country to independence. On March 6, 1957, the colony of the Gold Coast became the free nation of Ghana. Nkrumah served as president of Ghana from 1960 to 1966 and inspired many other Africans to fight to regain their independence. One by one during the 1950s and 1960s, Africans liberated their nations from European rule.

Source: Bankole Timothy, *Kwame Nkrumah—From Cradle to Grave*. Dorchester, Dorset, Great Britain: The Gavin Press Limited, 1981.

Long Walk To Freedom

by Nelson Mandela, 1994

In 1948 South Africa established a system of laws that enforced racial segregation known as apartheid. Nelson Mandela (b. 1918) is a black South African lawyer who led opposition to apartheid. In 1964 he was imprisoned for his opposition and was not released until 1990. Following are three excerpts from Mandela's autobiography. The first two tell of the hardships Mandela and other political prisoners faced. These hardships included forced labor under inhumane conditions and the denial of rights. Even reading a newspaper was forbidden. In the third excerpt Mandela reflects on his experiences after being released from prison. In the years following his imprisonment, Mandela continued working to tear down apartheid with the help of South African President F.W. DeKlerk. In the final excerpt Mandela says, "the truth is that we are not yet free." Why does he say that?

After arriving in the morning, we would fetch our picks, shovels, hammers, and wheelbarrows from a zinc shed at the top of the quarry. Then we would **array** ourselves along the quarry face, usually in groups of three or four. **Warders** with automatic weapons stood on raised platforms watching us. Unarmed warders walked among us, urging us to work harder. "*Gaan aan! Gaan aan!*" (Go on! Go on!), they would shout, as if we were oxen.

array: arrange
Warders: guards

By eleven, when the sun was high in the sky, we would begin to flag. By that time, I would already be drenched in sweat. The warders would then drive us even harder. "*Nee, man! Kom aan! Kom aan!*" (No, man! Come on! Come on!), they would shout. Just before noon, when we would break for lunch, we would pile the lime into wheelbarrows and cart it over to the truck, which would take it away....

Worse than the heat at the quarry was the light. Our backs were protected from the sun by our shirts, but the sun's rays would be reflected into our eyes by the lime itself. The glare hurt our eyes and, along with the dust, made it difficult to see. Our eyes teared and our faces became fixed in a permanent squint. It would take a long time after each day's work for our eyes to adjust to the **diminished** light.

diminished: decreased

After our first few days at the quarry, we made an official request for sunglasses. The authorities refused. This was not unexpected, for we were then not even permitted reading glasses. I had previously pointed out to the commanding officer that it did not make sense to permit us to read books but not permit us glasses to read them with.

During the following weeks and months, we requested sunglasses again and again. But it was to take us almost three years before we were allowed to have them, and that was only after a sympathetic physician agreed that the glasses were necessary to preserve our eyesight. Even then, we had to purchase the glasses ourselves.

For us, such struggles—for sunglasses, long trousers, study privileges, equalized food—were **corollaries to** the struggle we waged outside prison. The campaign to improve conditions in prison was part of the apartheid struggle. It was, in that sense, all the same; we fought injustice wherever we found it, no matter how large, or how small, and we fought injustice to preserve our own humanity….

corollaries to: natural results of

When I noticed the newspaper lying on the bench, I quickly left my cell, walked to the end of the corridor, looked in both directions, and then plucked the newspaper off the bench and slipped it into my shirt. Normally, I would have hidden the newspaper somewhere in my cell and taken it out only after bedtime. But like a child who eats his sweet before his main course, I was so eager for news that I opened the paper in my cell immediately.

I don't know how long I was reading; I was so **engrossed** in the paper that I did not hear any footsteps. Suddenly, an officer and two other warders appeared and I did not even have time to slide the paper under my bed. I was caught black-and-white-handed, so to speak. "Mandela," the officer said, "we are charging you for possession of **contraband**, and you will pay for this." The two warders then began a thorough search of my cell to see if they could turn up anything else.

engrossed: interested

Within a day or two a **magistrate** was brought in from Cape Town and I was taken to the room at headquarters that was used as the island's court. In this instance, the authorities were willing to call in an outside magistrate because they knew they had an open-and-shut case. I offered no defense, and was sentenced to three days in isolation and **deprivation of** meals….

contraband: smuggled goods

magistrate: government officer

The isolation cells were in our same complex, but in another wing. Although just across the courtyard, they felt enormously distant. In isolation, one was deprived of company, exercise, and even food: one received only rice water three times a day for three days. (Rice water is simply water in which rice has been boiled.) By comparison, our normal ration of **pap** seemed like a feast.

deprivation of: no

The first day in isolation was always the most painful. One grows accustomed to eating regularly and the body is not used to being deprived. I found that by the second day I had more or less adjusted to the absence of food, and the third passed without much craving at all.

pap: ground up food

Such deprivation was not uncommon among Africans in everyday life. I myself had gone without food for days at a time in my early years in Johannesburg.

As I have already mentioned, I found solitary confinement the most forbidding aspect of prison life. There is no end and no beginning; there is only one's own mind, which can begin to play tricks. Was that a dream or did it really happen? One begins to question everything. Did I make the right decision, was my sacrifice worth it? In solitary, there is no distraction from these haunting questions.

But the human body has an enormous capacity for adjusting to trying circumstances. I have found that one can bear the unbearable if one can keep one's spirits strong even when one's body is being tested. Strong **convictions** are the secret of surviving deprivation; your spirit can be full even when your stomach is empty....

convictions: beliefs

It was during those long and lonely years that my hunger for the freedom of my own people became a hunger for the freedom of all people, white and black. I knew as well as I knew anything that the **oppressor** must be liberated just as surely as the oppressed. A man who takes away another man's freedom is a prisoner of hatred, he is locked behind the bars of prejudice and narrow-mindedness. I am not truly free if I am taking away someone else's freedom, just as surely as I am not free when my freedom is taken from me. The oppressed and the oppressor alike are robbed of their humanity.

oppressor: one who controls with force

When I walked out of prison, that was my mission, to liberate the oppressed and the oppressor both. Some say that has now been achieved. But I know that that is not the case. The truth is that we are not yet free; we have merely achieved the freedom to be free, the right not to be oppressed. We have not taken the final step of our journey, but the first step on a longer and even more difficult road. For to be free is not merely to cast off one's chains, but to live in a way that respects and **enhances** the freedom of others. The true test of our devotion to freedom is just beginning.

enhances: improves the quality of

I have walked that long road to freedom. I have tried not to **falter**; I have made missteps along the way. But I have discovered the secret that after climbing a great hill, one only finds that there are many more hills to climb. I have taken a moment here to rest, to steal a view of the glorious **vista** that surrounds me, to look back on the distance I have come. But I can rest only for a moment, for with freedom comes responsibilities, and I dare not **linger**, for my long walk is not yet ended.

falter: hesitate

vista: view

linger: delay

Nelson Mandela and F.W. DeKlerk shared the 1993 Nobel Peace Prize for their work in ending apartheid. In 1994, black South Africans were allowed to vote in nationwide elections for the first time. Nelson Mandela was elected president of South Africa.

Source: Nelson Mandela, *Long Walk to Freedom: The Autobiography of Nelson Mandela.* Boston: Little, Brown and Co., 1994.

Amphibians In Danger, A Worldwide Warning

by Ron Fridell

Amphibians are the survivors of the natural world. They have lived on Earth for millions of years—longer than human beings. In fact, these small animals, including frogs, toads, and salamanders, have survived environmental changes that killed off most of the ocean life and the mighty dinosaurs—at least, until now. Today, amphibians all over the world are dying out and scientists want to know why. In this race against time, researchers are working to find the link in our natural world between changes in our environment and this potential amphibian extinction. How do factors such as global climate change, pollution, and the use of pesticides, endanger amphibians? What can we do to reverse these changes and save our planet?

With no scales, hair, or feathers to protect them, amphibians have more intimate contact with the environment than other animals do. They breathe in air and moisture through their thin, **permeable** skin, which reabsorbs chemicals from soil and water.

permeable: having pores or openings that permit gases or liquids to seep through

Amphibians are also exposed to more environments and more parts of any given environment than many other creatures. They can be found on every continent except Antarctica, and live in all sorts of places—from deserts to forests and from deep valleys to mountaintops. Most adult amphibians spend time on land and in the water. In addition, amphibians feed at different points on the food web at different times in their lives. As tadpoles, they consume plant matter; as adults, they eat insects.

Zoologist Henry Wilbur of Duke University has compared amphibians to canaries in coal mines. In the past, coal miners brought canaries with them into mine shafts. These small birds have delicate **respiratory systems**, so they are much more sensitive to toxic gases than people are. When a canary had trouble breathing—or died—miners knew the shaft was not safe and hurried to the surface. Amphibians are our canaries—they act as environmental monitors.

respiratory systems: a number of organs such as the lungs, windpipe, and diaphragm that serve the function of breathing

This is not to say that amphibians are not also hardy survivors. They've been around for hundreds of millions of years longer than we have. They survived whatever changes wiped out about 90 percent of all ocean species 250 million years ago. They lived through whatever forces drove the mighty dinosaurs to extinction 65 million years ago. We don't know exactly what caused the major extinctions of the past, but we do know that human activities are currently changing Earth's environment more rapidly than whatever caused the earlier extinctions.

These changes may be happening so fast that amphibians, and other creatures, cannot adapt quickly enough to survive. William Brown, science advisor to the secretary of the interior, sees it this way: "When species like frogs and toads that have been with us since the Jurassic period suddenly start to disappear—without us understanding exactly why—you have to take notice."

One of the suspects thought to be behind declining amphibian populations was closely linked with **UVB rays** and the eroding ozone shield. It was global climate change. Five of the 12 driest months on record and 6 of the 10 warmest years since 1855 occurred during the 1980s. The 1990s have been alarmingly warm too. In fact, 1995 is currently the warmest year in recorded history.

UVB rays: lines of light that cause sunburn

Once again, humans are to blame. For the past 200 years, we have been burning fossil fuels, such as coal, oil, gas, and cutting down and burning forests worldwide. This has brought about a steady increase in the levels of carbon dioxide, **methane**, and nitrous oxide in the atmosphere. Between 1958 and 1988, the amount of carbon dioxide in the atmosphere increased by 11 percent. Like the windows in a greenhouse, these gases—called greenhouse gases—trap heat from the sun.

methane: a gas with no color or odor used in cooking and heating

When sunlight hits Earth's surface, some of the energy is absorbed and the rest is reflected as infrared rays. Greenhouse gases in the atmosphere trap the infrared rays and combine with them to produce energy that heats up the atmosphere. This process is called the greenhouse effect.

For Earth's atmosphere to remain healthy, it must be balanced. In other words, the amount of energy going out and the amount of energy coming in must be equal. Our use of fossil fuels has upset this delicate balance. Scientific studies suggest that the concentration of greenhouse gases in the atmosphere is currently greater than at any other time in Earth's history. Today the average temperature on Earth's surface is 1° F (0.5°C) greater than it was a century ago. In 1995 alone, the average temperature on Earth rose 0.5° F (0.25°C). Many scientists believe that greenhouse gases are responsible for these increases. They predict that over the next century, average global temperatures will climb another 2 to 6° F (1 to 3°C).

As we burn more and more fossil fuels, the rate of climate change will accelerate. What sorts of global climate changes are scientists predicting?

- Earth will keep heating up due to the greenhouse effect.
- Weather patterns will become less and less predictable and more and more extreme.
- There will be more droughts worldwide, but there will also be more floods.

- Skies will become cloudier, and storms will become more frequent and extreme. There will be more rain worldwide, because the increase in air temperature leads to an increase in evaporation, which means more precipitation.
- More and more sea ice in the Arctic will melt. In recent scientific expeditions to the far north, researchers have found Arctic ice less than half as thick as expected. In addition, seawater was much less salty than expected because melting ice dilutes the ocean with fresh water. Scientists predict that in years to come the Arctic ice cap may melt entirely in summer. As the total volume of ice decreases, the rate of melting will increase. This is because ice reflects the sun's rays and open water absorbs them. As Arctic ice melts, sea levels will rise worldwide.
- Temperatures will **fluctuate** more radically and more unpredictably. There will be shifts in the growing season of plants and the active season of animals.
- Worldwide climate conditions will move more steadily northward and southward at a rate of 3 to 6 miles (4.8 to 9.6 km) per year. In other words, areas covered by temperate forests today will soon become more tropical.

fluctuate: to shift back and forth

What does all this mean to amphibians? Although a warmer world would benefit amphibians in some ways, too much of anything can be harmful or even fatal, especially to creatures as dependent on their surroundings as amphibians.

Amphibians are *cold-blooded*. Their body temperature changes with the temperature of the environment. A frog sitting on a warm rock will absorb the rock's heat heat and warm up; a frog sitting in a cold pond will cool down. On average, amphibians can tolerate temperatures ranging from 28 to 96°F (−2 to 36°C). This tolerance to a wide range of temperatures has enabled amphibians to live in so many different kinds of climates.

But there's a catch. Amphibians can adjust to temporary local changes, but they need overall conditions to remain relatively stable. Their delicate eggs and tadpoles will shrivel and die if ponds, streams, and pools suddenly dry up. Take the golden toads, for instance: In the two years immediately preceding their disappearance, rainfall in the Monteverde Cloud Reserve was unusually low. It is likely that many of the golden toads' seasonal breeding ponds dried up early, killing off their young.

Unfortunately, scientists don't know exactly how global climate change will affect amphibians and other creatures. They need to collect data over a longer period of time. Scientists face the same obstacle when it comes to another possible cause of amphibian decline—pollution.

When you hear the word *pollution*, you may picture factories dumping toxic waste into rivers; tankers leaking oil into oceans; farmers spraying their crops with pesticides; or cars, trucks and buses spewing exhaust fumes into the air over cities. The scientists at the 1990 emergency conference at Irvine knew that pollution was getting worse all over the planet, but they had very little data to tell them how it might be affecting amphibians. The data they did have strongly suggested that certain kinds of pollution, such as acid precipitation and pesticides, are at least partially responsible for the amphibian population decline.

Like UVB rays, acid rain and snow can affect amphibians in remote places that appear to be free of human activity. They develop when precipitation in the air mixes with pollutants, such as sulfur and nitrate from automobile exhaust and coal-burning factories, to produce sulfuric acid and nitric acid. The results of acid precipitation can be devastating. At least one-fifth of the forests of Europe and vast areas of forests in the northeastern United States and Canada have been hit hard by acid rain.

What does this mean to amphibians? For most species, it's bad news. Acid from acid precipitation accumulates in and around the lakes and ponds where amphibians live. Concentrations of acid are highest in early spring, when large quantities of rain fall and snow melts. Unfortunately, this puts newly laid amphibian eggs at risk. Melting acid snow can be especially deadly by producing an acid pulse—a sudden release of acid into the water—that acts like a dose of poison to amphibian eggs. Studies show that even slightly acidic water can kill the eggs of frogs and toads or result in deformed tadpoles. Salamanders are no better off. Acid precipitation has been blamed for the disappearance of tiger salamanders from parts of the Colorado Rockies.

Remember, amphibians are highly adaptable creatures, but they need time to adapt to new conditions. Expose them to sudden, human-made changes, such as acid pulses, and they will suffer.

The problems facing amphibians today may well face human beings in the future. The solutions found by scientists may one day save all of us.

Source: Ron Fridell, *Amphibians in Danger, A Worldwide Warning*. New York: Franklin Watts Publishing, 1999.

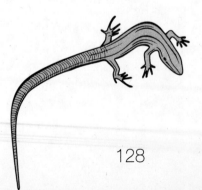

(continued from copyright page)

"The Legacy of Columbus," printed in THE COBBLESTONE MAGAZINE January 1992 Vol. 13 by Sarah Elder Hale. Copyright © 1992 Cobblestone Publishing, Inc., NH.

"Progress in Industry" from POORS MANUAL OF RAILROADS, 1887 advertisement for E.S. Greeley & Co., Manufacturers, Importers and Dealers in Railway and Telegraph Supplies (TPB). Reprinted by permission of General Research Division, The New York Public Library, Astor, Lennox and Tilden Foundations.

Excerpt from CLARA'S DIARY: AN AMERICAN GIRL IN MEIJI JAPAN by Clara A.N. Whitney, edited by M. William Steele and Tamiko Ichimata. Copyright © 1978 in Japan. Kodansha International Ltd. NY.

Excerpt from LONG WALK TO FREEDOM by Nelson Mandela. Copyright © 1994 by Nelson Rolihlahla Mandela. Little, Brown and Company, NY.

"From Mouse to Bat" from THE BIRD WHO CLEANS THE WORLD by Victor Montejo. Copyright© 1991 by Wallace Kaufman. All rights reserved, Curbstone Press.

"The War Years in Vietnam" from WHEN HEAVEN AND EARTH CHANGED PLACES by Le Ly Hayslip. Copyright © 1989 by Le Ly Hayslip and Charles Jay Wurts. Doubleday, a division of Bantam Douubleday Dell Publishing Group, Inc.

"The Vision That I See" from Ch. 10 "Nkrumah the Orator" from KWAME NKRUMAH; FROM CRADLE TO GRAVE by Bankole Timothy. Copyright © 1981 by Bankole Timothy. Gavin Press Limited.

Excerpt from ALL QUIET ON THE WESTERN FRONT by Erich Maria Remarque. "Im Weisen Nichts Neues." Copyright © 1928 by Ullstein A.G.; Copyright © renewed 1956, 1957, 1958 by Erich Maria Remarque. Published by Little, Brown and Company.

"The Aeneid" from THE AENEID FOR BOYS AND GIRLS retold by Alfred J. Church. Copyright © 1962 by Macmillan Publishing Company, NY.

"The Splendors of Hangzhou" from CHINESE CIVILIZATION AND SOCIETY by Patricia Buckley Ebrey. Copyright © 1981 by The Free Press.

"The Iliad" from THE CHILDREN'S HOMER; THE ADVENTURES OF ODYSSEUS AND THE TALE OF TROY by Padraic Colum. Copyright © 1946 by Padraic Colum and Willy Pogany.

"The Story of the Flood" from THE EPIC OF GILGAMESH translated by N.K. Sanders. Copyright © 1960, 1964, 1972 N.K. Sanders. Penguin Books Ltd.

"Praying at the Western Wall" from GAVRIEL AND JEMAL by Brent Ashabranner. Copyright © 1984 by Brent Ashabranner. G.P. Putnam's Sons, New York.

Excerpt from EASTER ISLAND: *The Mystery Solved* by Thor Heyerdahl. Copyright © 1989 by Thor Heyerdahl. Published by Random House, Inc.

Excerpt from THE TALE OF THE GENJI by Murasaki Shikbu, translated by Edward Seidensticker. Copyright © 1975 by Edward Seidensticker. Alfred A. Knopf, Inc.

"Notebooks from the Renaissance" from SELECTIONS FROM THE NOTEBOOKS OF LEONARDO DA VINCI edited with commentaries by Irma A. Richter. Copyright © 1952 by Oxford University Press.

"Working in the Mines" from VICTORIAN WOMEN: *A Documentary Account of Women's Lives in Nineteenth-Century England, France, and the United States* edited by Erma Olafson Hellerstein, Leslie Parker Hume and Karen M. Offen. Copyright © 1981 by the Board of Trustees of the Leland Stanford Junior University.

"A Pilgrimage to Mecca" from WE LIVE IN SAUDI ARABIA by Abdul Latif Al Hoad. Copyright © 1982 by Wayland Publishers, Ltd.

"Life of a Hindu Priest" from WE LIVE IN INDIA by Veen Sandal. Copyright © 1981. Published by Wayland Publishers, Ltd.

"Becoming a Buddhist Master" from WE LIVE IN MALAYSIA AND SINGAPORE by Jessie Wee. Copyright © 1984. Published by Wayland Publishers Ltd.

"A Craftsman in Bethlehem" from WE LIVE IN ISRAEL by Gemma Levine. Copyright © 1981. Published by Wayland Publishers Ltd.

"Letter from Jamaica" from SELECTED WRITINGS OF BOLIVAR compiled by Vicente Lecuaa, edited by Harold A. Bierck, Jr., translated by Lewis Bertrand. Volume 1, 1810-1822. Second edition published by the Bolivarian Society of Venezuela. Published by the Colonial Press Inc.

Headline from *The New York Times* "U. S. Attacked," September 12th, 2001. Reprinted by permission of *The New York Times,* NY.

Excerpt from AMPHIBIANS IN DANGER by Ron Fridell. Copyright © 1999 by Ron Fridell. Published by Franklin Watts, Danbury CT.

Excerpt from HATSHEPSUT by Catherine M. Andronik. Copyright © 2001 by Catherine M. Andronik. Published by Atheneum Books for Young Readers, NY.

Activities

Teachers share a common goal—to help their students become successful learners who can understand, remember, and apply important knowledge and skills. This important goal is best supported when students are offered a variety of ways in which to learn.

The Social Studies Anthology offers you the rich and varied tools that you need to help your students learn. It includes such diverse sources as diaries, poems, songs, stories, legends, and posters—all of which draw students into the sights and sounds of the places and times they are studying.

You may invite students to explore the Anthology selections in many unique ways—rewriting documents in another genre, dramatizing the selection, creating posters or collages, or writing original poems, stories, and songs. We have provided an activity for teaching each selection in the Anthology. But these activities, of course, are only suggestions. You should feel free to teach the selection in any way that you feel is best suited for your own classroom.

SEEING EARTH FROM SPACE
by Patricia Lauber, 1990
Pages 2–3

Use with Introduction

Objectives

- ❏ *Recognize how perspectives change when viewing Earth from space.*
- ❏ *Identify problems common to all cultures on Earth.*
- ❏ *Write a proposal about working together for the good of all on Earth.*

Writing a Proposal

After students have read the selection, have them think about what Earth looks like from space. (From space the planet seems small and fragile, boundaries are blurred, and effects of pollution are noticeable.) *What are problems that all cultures on Earth face?* (Environmental problems are common to all inhabitants of Earth, regardless of political or religious differences—loss of tropical forests is causing land erosion, oil slicks pollute the oceans, and so on.) Then ask students to consider how one's perspective might be changed by viewing Earth from space. (Responses will vary but should touch on the idea of the small size of Earth and that all people share the same environment.)

Have students write a proposal about working together to preserve the beautiful natural features of the planet. You may wish to have partners work together on the proposals. Proposals should take into account environmental problems all over the world. Encourage students to share their proposals with the class.

EASTER ISLAND
by Thor Heyerdahl, 1989
Pages 4–7

Use with Introduction

Objectives

- ❏ *Investigate Thor Heyerdahl's theory of the technology that produced the statues of Easter Island.*
- ❏ *Recognize how archaeologists uncover facts about the past.*
- ❏ *Create a mural illustrating the carving and moving of a statue.*

Creating a Mural

Before students begin reading, explain that the selection tells how anthropologist Thor Heyerdahl investigated a puzzling history mystery on Easter Island that he could not easily explain. By searching for clues, just as archaeologists do, he discovered a possible solution to the mystery.

As students read the selection, encourage them to picture the scenes that Thor Heyerdahl describes. Tell students that they are going to create a mural, or wall-sized illustration, that illustrates the process of making and moving the *moai*. Divide the class into five groups and assign each a different step in the process—the opening ceremony, the tools and process of carving, the singing and feasting before moving the *moai*, the "walking" of the *moai*, and the setting up of the *moai* in its resting place. Have each group meet to discuss how to illustrate its step of the process and make up a list of pictorial elements that illustrate it. You may wish to borrow a copy of *Easter Island* by Thor Heyerdahl from the library for students to use as a visual reference.

Spread a long length of butcher paper on the floor of the classroom. Assign each group a portion of the paper and have them draw or paint their scenes on it to create an Easter Island mural. Display the completed mural on a wall of the classroom.

OLD STONE AGE CAVE PAINTINGS

about 18,000 B.C.
Page 9

Use with Chapter 1, Lesson 1

Objectives

❑ *Recognize the archaeological significance of the Stone Age cave paintings.*

❑ *Understand how archaeologists use such discoveries to learn about the people who lived during a particular time.*

❑ *Write a description of the cave paintings.*

Background Information

The discovery of Old Stone Age cave paintings throughout southwestern Europe has enriched our understanding of the life and culture of the peoples of this time. The paintings show bison, mammoths, woolly rhinoceroses, panthers, owls, and even hyenas. Archaeologists are unsure why the paintings were made. However, they do know that the paintings are rich in detail, indicating the artists' understanding of symbolism. This points to the ability to think in complex ways.

Writing a Description

After students have had a chance to look at the cave painting, ask them to discuss what they see. Then encourage students to discuss what such paintings reveal about the people who drew them. (The people had developed tools and skills for drawing and painting; they thought it was important to represent a part of their lives and preserve it in some way through art.) *Why was the discovery so important?* (It helps us to further understand life in the Old Stone Age.)

Have students write a description of the cave painting. Encourage students to share their descriptions with the class.

FIRST FRUITS OF THE FIELD

Kabyle Legend, retold by Anne Pellowski, 1990
Pages 10–11

Use with Chapter 1, Lesson 3

Objectives

❑ *Recognize the characteristics that make this story a legend.*

❑ *Appreciate the significance of agriculture in the course of human history.*

❑ *Write a description of early farming.*

Writing a Description

After students have read the selection, discuss with them what they know about legends. Point out that a **legend** is a story that explains how something came to be, often something in nature. In every culture legends are passed down from generation to generation, by word of mouth or by writing. This particular legend is from North Africa. Ask students what event this legend explains. (how people came to grow their own food) *What is the growing of plants and the raising of animals called?* (agriculture) Then ask students what character in the legend explained how to grow plants and animals. (an ant) *What did the First Parents need to know about in terms of growing crops.* (They needed to know about the importance of water for growing crops and for cooking the food that was raised.)

Have students write descriptions of early farming. Encourage them to conduct further research about farming during ancient times using encyclopedias and other reference sources. Students can share their descriptions with the class.

THE EPIC OF GILGAMESH

Sumerian Epic, 3000–2000 B.C.
Page 12

Use with Chapter 2, Lesson 2

Objectives

- ❏ *Explore the world's oldest epic.*
- ❏ *Illustrate an epic.*

Background Information

The Epic of Gilgamesh is named for a legendary king of the Sumerian city of Uruk, who may have lived in about 2700 B.C. Uruk, which is referred to as Erech in the Bible, was located on the Euphrates River near the modern city of Warka, Iraq. *The Epic of Gilgamesh* was preserved by many later Mesopotamian peoples who added to and modified the story. The story of the flood was probably added to *The Epic of Gilgamesh* by a later people. No one knows for certain when this occurred, but it was probably based on an independent tradition of flood stories that were widespread in ancient Mesopotamia.

Illustrating an Epic

After students have read the selection, discuss the background information with them. Ask students: *What is the overall tone of this story?* (Students may suggest that it is an emotional and tragic story since human beings are "turned to clay," or destroyed, although the narrator survives.)

Have students create illustrations of different portions of the story that reflect its dramatic tone. Explain to students that, according to the epic, the deck of the boat was a 120-cubit-long square and took up an acre. (A cubit is the distance from fingertip to elbow.) There were six decks below the main one, and the boat held all of the narrator's large household as well as "the beast of the field, both wild and tame." Students may wish to look up Sumerian art in the encyclopedia or the library to get an idea of what Sumerian clothes were like. Have students display their work around the classroom.

PRAYING AT THE WESTERN WALL

by Brent Ashabranner, 1984
Pages 13–14

Use with Chapter 2, Lesson 4

Objectives

- ❏ *Identify religious traditions.*
- ❏ *Recognize how religious traditions can bind people together.*
- ❏ *Write a report about a Jewish tradition.*

Writing a Report

After students have read the selection, ask them to discuss the traditions of Judaism that are described in the selection. (praying at the Western Wall, bar mitzvah, tefillin, mezuzah, songs on Shabbat or Passover) *How do such traditions bind families together?* (Point out how bonds grow from our shared traditions.)

Then have students work in small groups to research a religious tradition that they know about and report to the class. Groups of five can work together to write their reports.

THE ROSETTA STONE
Egyptian Decree, 196 B.C.
Pages 15–16

Use with Chapter 3, Lesson 2

Objectives
- ❏ *Understand how the Rosetta Stone enabled scholars to decipher Egyptian hieroglyphics.*
- ❏ *Write and read hieroglyphic writing.*

Background Information

The Rosetta Stone was discovered in 1799 by French soldiers. They were part of an army commanded by Napoleon Bonaparte that had invaded Egypt the year before. Soldiers were digging trenches near the town of Rosetta when they dug up a large black stone covered with three kinds of writing. Scholars read the Greek inscription easily and were able to use it to decipher the demotic and hieroglyphic inscriptions on the stone.

Writing and Reading Hieroglyphic Writing

Ask students if any of them have worked with rebus puzzles. If possible, demonstrate a sample of rebus writing for the class. Tell students that rebus writing is somewhat similar to hieroglyphic writing. Like a rebus symbol, a hieroglyphic sign can sometimes represent an object whose name is part of a larger word that means something different. Hieroglyphic signs can also stand for ideas. For example, a picture of a man carrying something could mean "carrying." Some hieroglyphic signs help explain other signs. For instance, a sign shaped like an eye might indicate that another sign nearby has to do with seeing. Have students look at the pictures of hieroglyphic writing and identify signs that look like people or familiar objects such as birds.

After students have read the selection, have them use the symbols that are explained in the selection to write one or two hieroglyphic sentences on a piece of paper—for example, "Strength gave him victory." Then have them exchange papers with a classmate and try to read each other's sentence(s).

HATSHEPSUT, HIS MAJESTY, HERSELF
by Catherine M. Andronik
Pages 17–19

Use with Chapter 3, Lesson 3

Objectives
- ❏ *Identify the events that led to Hatshepsut becoming pharaoh of Egypt.*
- ❏ *Understand the importance of Hatshepsut's rule.*
- ❏ *Write an obituary for Hatshepsut.*

Rewriting in Another Genre

After the selection has been read, point out to students that Hatshepsut was one of Egypt's few female pharaohs. Ask students: *How was she treated as a child by her father, Pharaoh Tuthmosis?* (He included her in activities intended for men and boys, such as hunting crocodiles.) *Whom did she marry and what happened to him?* (She married her half-brother, who died a few years after his coronation.) *What were her duties as regent?* (She ruled the country until her nephew was old enough to be crowned pharaoh.) *How did Hatshepsut become pharaoh?* (She had herself crowned at some point during her rule.) Encourage students to discuss the importance of Hatshepsut's reign. Ask: *Why was Hatshepsut a good ruler?* (She made important political decisions. She was powerful and influential.) *Why was the concept of* maat *important to the Egyptian people?* (It signified a sense of cosmic order and righteousness, that related to the will of the gods.) *Why do you think the author called this biography,* Hatshepsut, His Majesty, Herself? (The title emphasizes her important role as a pharaoh, a role generally assumed by men.)

Provide small groups of students with current newspaper and magazine obituaries. Encourage them to study the obituaries to understand the kinds of information to include. Invite these groups to brainstorm the characteristics of a well-written obituary. Then, ask students to do additional research about Hatshepsut's life, using classroom encyclopedias and the Internet. Have each student write an obituary for the Egyptian pharaoh that might appear in a contemporary newspaper. Have volunteers share their work with the class.

HOWARD CARTER'S DIARY
Pages 20–21

Use with Chapter 3, Lesson 3

Objectives

❑ *Appreciate the value of reading a first-person account of an important historical event.*

❑ *Understand the significance of Howard Carter's great discovery.*

❑ *Role-play an interview.*

Role-Playing an Interview

After students have read the selection, remind them that the text is a first-person account by Howard Carter, describing what he first saw when he peered into one of the chambers of King Tut's tomb. Ask: *How is reading a first-person account different from reading a description of the same event by a modern day writer who was not at the scene?* (It is more exciting to read Carter's first-person account. Carter would know details that another writer wouldn't.) *What do you think historians and archaeologists have learned about ancient Egypt as a result of this discovery?* (The objects showed the value that pharaohs placed on different possessions. The tomb's contents also presented a picture of the lifestyle of an Egyptian ruler. Also, we now know more about the techniques used by Egyptian artists and artisans.) *Which of the objects described in the selection would you like to see?* (Answers will vary.) *Do you think archaeologists should disturb the burial places of ancient people?* (Answers will vary.)

Have pairs of students role-play an interview between Howard Carter and a newspaper reporter from the period about the discovery of King Tut's tomb. Students should do additional research about Carter's discovery, using classroom encyclopedias and the Internet. After completing their research, student teams should prepare at least five questions and answers for the role-play. Ask students to take turns playing the parts of Howard Carter and the reporter. Then call on pairs of students to present their role-plays in class. Invite other students to ask additional questions.

LIFE OF A HINDU PRIEST
by Hardwari Lal, 1984
Pages 22–23

Use with Chapter 4, Lesson 3

Objectives

❑ *Recognize religious traditions.*

❑ *Identify the religious duties of a Hindu priest.*

❑ *Create a log of a Hindu priest's daily duties.*

Creating a Log

Discuss with students how important religion is in the lives of the Hindus of India. Ask students what distinctive features of Hinduism Hardwari Lal describes. (Responses will vary but should mention 330 million deities, large number of idols, and grand ceremonies.) Then ask students to talk about what the daily life of a Hindu priest is like.

Have students research the duties of another religious leader such as a Jewish rabbi, a Catholic priest, or a Protestant minister. Then ask students to write a log or record of one day in the life of a religious leader. After students have completed their logs, encourage them to compare what they wrote.

BECOMING A BUDDHIST MASTER
by Sek Bao Shi, 1985
Pages 24–25

Use with Chapter 4, Lesson 4

Objectives

- ❑ *Recognize religious traditions.*
- ❑ *Identify the process through which a person becomes a Buddhist master.*
- ❑ *Write a story about the life of a Buddhist master based on the selection.*

Writing a Story

After students have read the selection, ask them to discuss why they think so much discipline is involved in becoming a Buddhist master. (Such a disciplined life enables the person who is seeking to become a master to be more open to Buddha's teachings.) Then ask students to talk about why the Buddhists in the temple are vegetarians. (They do not believe in harming any living creature.)

Have students write a story about Sek Bao Shi or a leader from another religion with which they are familiar. Students may also be interested in conducting research to add details to their stories.

THE TERRA COTTA ARMY OF EMPEROR QIN
by Caroline Lazo
Pages 26–27

Use with Chapter 5, Lesson 3

Objectives

- ❑ *Recognize the role played by archaeologists in helping us learn about our past.*
- ❑ *Write a diary entry.*

Writing a Diary Entry

After students have read the selection, have them discuss the significant role of archaeologists in uncovering important clues about the way people lived long ago. Explain that archaeologists are scientists who examine objects made hundreds or even thousands of years ago, such as tools, pottery, tombs, clothing, and jewelry. By using special methods and equipment(everything from simple shovels and brushes to computers), they study these artifacts to find out about the cultures of ancient civilizations. Ask: *What do you think archaeologists will learn by studying these terra cotta figures?* (They will learn about the techniques used to make the sculptures, the appearance of ancient Chinese soldiers, and the way people lived and worked in ancient China.) *What have we learned by studying the ancient, historical records that describe the tomb?* (how many people worked there; what the contents looked like; what the artisans, who worked on the tomb site, created; what happened to the artisans.) *Why do you think the Chinese government is now permitting archaeologists to excavate ancient burial places?* (They view them as valuable teaching tools and as examples of China's heritage.)

Invite students to do more research about the figures, using classroom encyclopedias and the Internet. Encourage students to write a diary entry by an American visitor who has just seen the statues. Remind them that diary entries are written in the first person. Call on volunteers to share their entries with the rest of the class.

A LETTER FROM A HAN EMPEROR

by Emperor Wen Ti, about 160 B.C.
Page 28

Use with Chapter 5, Lesson 4

Objectives

❏ *Recognize that historically many world leaders have worked for peaceful solutions.*

❏ *Identify the diversity that existed in China in ancient times.*

❏ *Write a letter to the emperor.*

Writing a Letter

After students have read the selection, discuss why the letter was significant. (It was written by the emperor of China, who was urging the people of the northern steppes and the people of the House of Han to live together in peace.) Ask students to describe how the people to the north of the wall were different from the people south of the wall. (The people to the north were hunters who used bows and arrows to hunt their food, while the people south of the wall were engaged in agriculture and the manufacture of cloth.)

Have students write a letter to the emperor from the captain of the people of the northern steppes. How will he reply to the emperor of China? You may wish to brainstorm ideas with the whole class before they write their letters.

THE ILIAD

by Homer, about the 8th century B.C.
Pages 30–32

Use with Chapter 6, Lesson 2

Objectives

❏ *Recognize the excerpt from Homer's The Iliad as a part of a classic work of ancient Greek literature.*

❏ *Identify recurring themes in Greek mythology that appear in the selection.*

❏ *Construct a fuller account of Achilles' role in The Iliad.*

Building Knowledge

Indicate to students that they are going to read an excerpt from one of the oldest and most famous examples of European literature—Homer's *The Iliad*. Help them get a sense of just how long ago it was written—over 2,500 years ago. Then have them read the excerpt. After they have finished, discuss the idea that Greek mythology focuses on mortal heroes, gods and goddesses, and on relations between mortals and gods. Ask students: *Who is the hero of this tale?* (Achilles) *In what way was he involved with gods and goddesses? How did they help him?* Help students to see how closely intertwined the lives of mortals and gods were in ancient Greek literature—mortals could even have gods as parents, as Achilles did in Thetis, and gods could intercede for and directly help mortals, just as Thetis and Hephaistos helped Achilles. Help students to recognize the tone of tragedy that is a common feature of Greek mythology.

Point out to the class that there is much more to the Achilles legend than appears in this excerpt. Have them do research to find out how Hector and Achilles met their ends and the origin of the term *Achilles' heel*. Tell students to write their own expanded accounts of the story.

144

THE BIRDS
by Aristophanes, 414 B.C.
Pages 33–34

Use with Chapter 6, Lesson 3

Objectives

❑ *Recognize that the play entertains as well as provides information about life in Athens.*

❑ *Identify how Aristophanes used satire in his plays.*

❑ *Write a review of the play.*

Writing a Review

After students have read the excerpt from *The Birds*, discuss why Aristophanes wrote the play. (to protest Athens's war with Sicily) Then remind students that **satire** is a special form of humor often used to ridicule human vices and follies. Ask students what elements of satire they can find in the play. (choice of birds to represent the perfect Athenians, building a walled city between Heaven and Earth so that the Sicilians cannot get over it) *Are satires still written today? Do playwrights still write plays to protest events?* (Responses will vary, but students should be aware that satire is still used as a literary device and that plays are sometimes written to protest political events.)

Have students write a review of the play as if they had attended a performance. Did it effectively protest the war? Was the humor apparent? You may wish to have partners work together to write their reviews.

ATLANTIS, THE LEGEND OF A LOST CITY
retold by Christine Balit
Pages 35–37

Use with Chapter 6, lesson 3

Objectives

❑ *Evaluate a famous legend.*

❑ *Illustrate a legend.*

Illustrating a Legend

After students have read the selection, encourage them to discuss the story. Begin by asking them to compare this selection to others they have read. Then ask: *What does this legend describe?* (the creation and destruction of the island of Atlantis) *How does Poseidon's commandment affect the lives of the citizens of Atlantis?* (By requiring that no person should take up arms against another, the people became kind and gentle and lived peacefully. The city prospered.) *How did the people of Atlantis eventually change?* (They became ambitious and greedy. They began to cheat and steal. The city became dangerous.) *What was the result of their behavior?* (Poseidon punished them by causing Atlantis to be swallowed up in the sea.) *What do you think is the moral of this story?* (The quest for power and ambition destroys goodness and kindness and ultimately is self-destructive.)

Divide the class into small groups and encourage students to discuss the moods or feelings created by this legend. Encourage groups to identify the key scenes in the story. Then, distribute drawing paper and supplies. Ask each student to divide the drawing paper into four equal squares. Have students create four illustrations of different parts of the story that reflect these important dramatic events and the tone or mood of each. Have students display their work in class.

THE AENEID
by Virgil, 19 B.C.
Pages 38–39

Use with Chapter 7, Lesson 3

Objectives

❑ *Sample a classic of ancient Roman literature—Virgil's Aeneid.*

❑ *Draw inferences from the Aeneid about what people valued in ancient Rome.*

❑ *Rewrite an episode from the Aeneid as a news story.*

Rewriting in Another Genre

After students have read the selection, help them to draw inferences about the society it treats. Ask students such questions as: *What does the way that King Acestes greeted Aeneas tell you about the ancient Romans' attitude toward visitors?* (They believed that showing hospitality was important.) *What does Aeneas's remembrance of his father reveal?* (that respect and honor were due to one's ancestors) *What do the games and how they were run tell you about Roman society's values?* (that they highly valued competition, winning, and prizes) *How did their sense of fair play differ from our own?* (They considered Nisus's cheating to be acceptable behavior.) *What does the Aeneid tell us about ancient Roman religious beliefs?* (that the Romans believed in omens, or signs from the gods)

Have students imagine that they are sports reporters sent to cover the games described in the *Aeneid.* Have them describe the events in the form of a news story for the sports pages. If possible, have newspaper clippings of sports stories available for students to use as models.

THE ERUPTION OF MOUNT VESUVIUS
by Pliny the Younger, A.D. 79
Page 40

Use with Chapter 7, Lesson 3

Objectives

❑ *Recognize the effect of natural disasters on ancient civilizations.*

❑ *Identify the significance of primary sources to the study of history.*

❑ *Write a news report about the eruption.*

Writing a News Report

After students have read the selection, discuss what effect the eruption had on the people of Pompeii. (Many lost their lives, and many lost their homes and belongings.) *Why was it difficult for them to escape?* (Although there had been some earth tremors, the people were not alarmed and did not have sufficient warning to make their escape.) Point out that the people were so frightened by this natural phenomenon that they thought the gods had been killed and that the end of the world had come. Remind students that this selection is a primary source, that is, it was written by someone who actually experienced the event. Ask students why primary sources are so valuable to the study of history. (They give us first-hand descriptions of actual events.)

Have students write a news report about the eruption. Remind them to tell *who, what, when, where, why,* and *how* in their reports. You may wish to create a bulletin-board display of students' reports along with some illustrations of Vesuvius.

A CRAFTSMAN IN BETHLEHEM
by Avram Hissan, 1981
Pages 41–42

Use with Chapter 7, Lesson 4

Objectives

- ❏ *Identify religious traditions.*
- ❏ *Understand how religion has shaped the life of Avram Hissan, a Christian who lives in Bethlehem.*
- ❏ *Build knowledge about modern-day Bethlehem.*

Building Knowledge

After students have read the selection, discuss the importance of Bethlehem in the religious traditions of Christians. (According to the New Testament, Bethlehem was the birthplace of Jesus.) Then discuss with students what kinds of crafts Avram Hissan makes. (He creates religious articles from olive wood and mother of pearl for the many tourists and religious pilgrims who come to Bethlehem.)

In the selection Hissan mentions that Muslims, Jews, and Christians have long lived together in Bethlehem. Have students conduct some research about modern-day Bethlehem to find out what the city is like today and the role it plays in the current events of the area. Encourage students to share their findings with the class.

FROM MOUSE TO BAT
Maya Fable, retold by Victor Montejo, 1991
Pages 43–44

Use with Chapter 8, Lesson 2

Objectives

- ❏ *Interpret the moral of the fable.*
- ❏ *Write a fable with a moral.*

Writing Your Own Fable

Remind the class of the many cultures that have fables that include morals. (for example, *Aesop's Fables*, which were first told among the ancient Greeks) Tell students that they are going to read a fable from another civilization—that of the Maya.

After students have read the fable, help them to identify its theme of discontent with one's condition and explore it with them. Ask students: *Why was Tx'ow discontented? What did he do about it?* (He thought he deserved more than he had; he convinced the other mice that they also deserved more.) *What did his discontent get him?* (the chance for a change, but not necessarily for an improvement in his lot) *What would you say the moral of the fable is?* (Encourage all reasonable answers; possible answers include: Be satisfied with your lot—it could be worse; Don't count your chickens before they are hatched—the change that you are sure will be for the better may be for the worse.) As students suggest different morals, list them on the chalkboard. Then encourage them to suggest other morals with which they are familiar, such as "A stitch in time saves nine" or "Pride goeth before a fall." Finally, have each student choose a moral and write his or her own fable about it.

PILGRIMAGE TO MECCA
by Samaan bin Jabir Al Nasaib, 1987
Pages 45–46

Use with Chapter 9, Lesson 2

Objectives

- ❏ *Identify religious traditions.*
- ❏ *Recognize the pilgrimage to Mecca as a significant Muslim religious event.*
- ❏ *Write a description of the pilgrimage.*

Writing a Description

After students have read the selection, discuss the "five pillars of Islam" with them. (the pilgrimage; a belief in one god; prayer five times a day; the giving of alms, or aid to the poor; and fasting during the holy month of Ramadan) Point out that the Islamic religion teaches that all Muslims should try to make the pilgrimage to Mecca once in their lifetime. Then have students recount what happens during the pilgrimage and discuss why great physical stamina is required. (Pilgrims often journey long distances to Mecca and once there must engage in rituals such as washing, prayer, walking, and running.)

Have students write a description of what happens once the pilgrims reach Mecca. Students may write their description as a list of events, or they may write a paragraph describing the events. Encourage students to discuss the events in their small groups.

AN ISLAMIC HOSPITAL
by Abd-ul-Wáhid al-Marrakhshi, about 1200
Page 47

Use with Chapter 9, Lesson 3

Objectives

- ❏ *Recognize the contributions made by Islamic civilization in the area of medical care.*
- ❏ *Link the selection to current events by writing an editorial about universal medical care.*

Linking to Current Events

After students have read the selection, encourage them to think about how this hospital was historically significant. *What did the hospital look like? What was provided for the patients? Whom did the hospital serve?* (The hospital was beautifully decorated with sculpture and tree-filled grounds, and the rooms had flowing water; the patients were given a daily ration of food, medicines, and clothing; the hospital served both the rich and the poor.) Point out that the patients who needed money were given some when they left the hospital and that the Prince of Marrakesh visited the patients every Friday. Ask students to compare and contrast this hospital with hospitals of today.

Have students write an editorial supporting or opposing universal medical care today. Tell them to be sure to include reasons to support their viewpoint. Encourage students to share their editorials with the class.

TORTOISE, HARE, AND THE SWEET POTATOES
retold by Ashley Bryan
Page 50–52

Use with Chapter 10, Lesson 1

Objectives

❑ *Recognize the characteristics of a folk tale.*

❑ *Identify the lesson of this folk tale.*

❑ *Write a folk tale.*

Writing Your Own Folk Tale

After students have read the selection, remind them that folk tales are part of an oral storytelling tradition typical of cultures all over the world. Invite students to discuss other folk tales they have read and compare them to this selection. Focus on the characteristics that are common to all folk tales, such as the use of animal characters, teaching a moral lesson, and entertaining readers or listeners. Ask: *How are the characters of Tortoise and Hare different?* (Tortoise is opposed to stealing. Hare is a thief and a trickster. Tortoise is wise, Hare is sly, but he can be tricked.)*Why do you think Tortoise agrees to steal the sweet potatoes with Hare?* (It is part of her plan to trick him.) *How does Tortoise outsmart Hare?* (She crawls into the sack and eats the sweet potatoes while Hare runs away.) *What lesson does this folk tale teach?* (Greed and deceit are punished in the end.)

Divide the class into small groups. Encourage the students to brainstorm an idea for a folk tale that teaches a lesson about greed. The main characters should be animals who behave like human beings. Have students write the folk tale as a group. Invite a representative from each group to read the folk tale to the class. Bind the stories in a book and display it in the classroom.

AÏDA
retold by Leontyne Price
Pages 53–56

Use with Chapter 10, Lesson 2

Objectives

❑ *Identify the conflicts faced by the different characters in this story.*

❑ *Dramatize a scene from the story.*

Dramatizing a Scene From the Story

After students have read the selection, show them the location of Egypt and Ethiopia on a classroom map or globe. Point out that although this story is fictional, it takes place in countries that have rich, and ancient cultures. Encourage students to discuss the conflicts, or struggles, faced by different story characters. Explain that these conflicts either can be internal, when characters struggle with their own emotions, or can involve other story characters or situations. Ask: *What personal conflict does Aïda face after she is enslaved in Egypt?* (She falls in love with Radames, who leads the Egyptian army against Ethiopia.) *Why do you think that Aïda shouts that Radames should be victorious?* (She was carried away by the cries of the crowd.) *What conflict does Radames face?* (He loves Aïda, but must marry the Pharaoh's daughter.) *What conflict does the Pharaoh's daughter face with Aïda?* (She is jealous when she realizes that Aïda loves Radames.) *What personal conflict does the Ethiopian King face when he sees his daughter again in Egypt?* (He cannot reveal that he is the King.) *Why do you think he asks Aïda not to betray him?* (He knows he will be killed if the Egyptians realize who he is; he has a better chance of asking for mercy for the conquered Ethiopians.)

Divide the class into small groups. Invite each group to choose a scene from the story to dramatize. Students can play the parts of different story characters, while one student can read the story narration. Other students in the group can contribute to the dramatization by acting as the director, writer, and costume person. Suggest that students add additional, original dialogue to the scene if necessary. Invite different groups to present their dramatizations in class. If video equipment is available, tape the presentation and play back the tape for the class.

MANSA MUSA
by Khephra Burns
Pages 57–61

Use with Chapter 10, Lesson 3

Objectives

- ❏ *Locate the country of Mali on a map.*
- ❏ *Understand the characters of Kankan and Tariq.*
- ❏ *Illustrate a scene from the story.*

Illustrating a Scene

After students have read the selection, ask them to identify Mali on a map or globe. Explain that centuries ago the western African nation was part of the great Mali empire. It is a landlocked country in the Sahara Desert. Ask: *What are Kankan's impressions of the desert in this story?* (When he first sees the desert, he thinks that the world has disappeared because it looks so different from his familiar village.) *When the stranger who visits his village talks about "the great sea to the west," what is he referring to?* (the Atlantic Ocean) Encourage students to discuss their reactions to Kankan's experiences in this story. Ask: *How does Kankan react when he listens to the stranger who visits his village?* (He is interested in what he says about the world beyond his village that he has never seen.) *What is his reaction to being kidnapped by the slave raiders?* (Although he is frightened, he vows to escape.) *What can you conclude about his character from his reaction to his kidnapping?* (He is brave and independent.) *How does he feel when he realizes that the traveler has bought him from his kidnappers?* (He is sad because he knows that he is a slave.) *What does Kankan's decision not to attack Tariq show about his character?* (He is wise not to attack him, because he could never survive alone in the desert.) *Based on his treatment of Kankan, what kind of person is Tariq?* (He seems wise and kind.) *What do you think Tariq means when he says to Kankan, "The journey is long, but it can only be made one step at a time."?* (He is referring to Kankan's journey through life.)

Have students work individually to illustrate one of the scenes from the story. Encourage them to research the setting by using encyclopedias, the Internet, and books about African history in their school library. Invite students to share their illustrations with the class.

TALE OF KING ARTHUR
retold by Sir James Knowles, 1923
Pages 62–65

Use with Chapter 11, Lesson 2

Objectives

- ❏ *Sample a well-known legend handed down from medieval times.*
- ❏ *Learn about medieval customs as described in the legend.*
- ❏ *Dramatize the legend of King Arthur.*

Background Information

The first stores about King Arthur probably involved a fifth-century Celtic warrior chief who fought against invading Saxon tribes. These early legends were very different from those we are familiar with today and included exploits such as leading an attack on the Celtic underworld. The legend of King Arthur began to resemble its modern form around the twelfth century, when it became mixed with other legends about British history and the search for a magical grail. This selection is from a twentieth-century retelling of the legend, which includes most of the elements with which we are familiar today.

Dramatizing the Legend

Introduce the legend by naming King Arthur and asking what students know about him. Then propose that they dramatize the legend of King Arthur, based on this selection. Divide the class into groups—one to create the script, another the props, another the scenery, another to be the narrators and actors (and, if time and materials are available, another to create costumes). You will need a director, too, perhaps yourself. Then have students read the selection, keeping in mind what their parts in dramatizing it will be.

Although the legend does not take place at a particular point in medieval history, encourage students to fix an approximate date and do some research about medieval customs. When the class has pulled its dramatization together and rehearsed it, invite another class in for the performance or present it at an assembly.

A CONTRACT BETWEEN A VASSAL AND A LORD
Contract from the 7th Century
Page 66

Use with Chapter 11, Lesson 2

Objectives

❑ *Explore the nature of a contract from the Middle Ages.*

❑ *Recognize the relationship that existed between lord and vassal.*

❑ *Write a contract.*

Writing Your Own Contract

First discuss with the class what a contract is—a binding agreement between parties in which each promises the other something. Then have students take turns reading this contract aloud. Have students pause as they encounter any difficult terms. Have them identify what each party to the contract pledges the other and what he expects in return. Ask students: *What does the vassal get from the lord?* (food, clothing, protection) *What does the lord get from the vassal?* (service)

Have students work in pairs to write a contract between a student and a teacher. Tell them to include what a teacher expects from a student and what a student expects from his or her teacher.

NOTEBOOKS FROM THE RENAISSANCE
by Leonardo da Vinci, about 1482–1519
Pages 67–69

Use with Chapter 11, Lesson 4

Objectives

❑ *Recognize Leonardo da Vinci as one of the world's best-known artists.*

❑ *Appreciate how da Vinci made broad knowledge the basis for his art and ideas.*

❑ *Create a da Vinci collage.*

Creating a Collage

Explain to the class that da Vinci is called a "Renaissance man," that is, a person who knows a great deal about a wide variety of subjects. Leonardo da Vinci was therefore exemplary of the burst of learning that took place during the Renaissance. Encourage students to examine his accomplishments as treated in the Anthology and discuss each one. Ask students *What areas of knowledge did da Vinci obviously explore deeply?* (art, anatomy, the laws of motion, and other physical laws) Help students to see how he used his knowledge to bring reality and movement to his art and to create far-seeing inventions.

Divide the class into groups and tell each group to create a collage presenting a cross section of da Vinci's work. Encourage students to find further examples of his work in the library and to either reproduce them or draw copies of them. Then have the groups use their selections to make collages for classroom display.

THE SPLENDORS OF HANGZHOU

by an Unknown Chinese Traveler, 1235
Pages 70–72

Use with Chapter 12, Lesson 3

Objectives

- ❏ *Recognize the richness and variety of a Chinese city over 700 years ago.*
- ❏ *Create illustrations that show its wonders.*

Creating Illustrations

As students read this selection, encourage them to try to picture the scenes they are reading about. When they have read the selection, ask them if the scenes described remind them of any places they know today. (perhaps malls or street fairs or kinds of entertainment they have seen, like circuses featuring acrobatic acts)

Divide the class into five groups. Assign to each group one of the parts of the selection—Markets, Commercial Establishments, Entertainment Centers, Boats, and Specialty Stores. Have each group create a poster-sized illustration of the sights described by the unknown author. Encourage students to do art research so as to depict the citizens and city of Hangzhou of the 1200s as authentically as possible. Students should divide the responsibilities for planning, researching, and drawing the different goods, places, and people to be seen in Hangzhou.

THE TALE OF GENJI

by Murasaki Shikibu, early 1000s
Pages 73–74

Use with Chapter 12, Lesson 5

Objectives

- ❏ *Sample part of a Japanese novel of 1,000 years ago.*
- ❏ *Perform the tale in Readers Theater.*

Using Readers Theater

This tale lends itself well to the technique of Readers Theater, in which students take the roles of characters and read their lines with expression. They do not mime the action but convey it with their oral interpretation.

Turning this tale into a reading script calls for appointing a director (you may want to act as director), naming one or more narrators, and casting the different roles (Genji, several of his retainers, and fisherfolk). You may want to change some of the paragraphs describing what Genji is doing to lines that he speaks himself. For example, you might want to change "Genji thought he could see. . . " to "I thought I could see. . . " or "Genji offered prayers. . . ", to "I offered prayers. . . "

Following the performance, hold a discussion of the tale among the performers and the audience. Encourage both groups to speculate about the meaning of the events in the selection. For example, ask students: *What could have been the reason for the dangerous storm?* (Perhaps the king of the sea sent the storm to show his displeasure with Genji for ignoring a summons.) *What do you think Genji might have done next?* Use questions such as these to explore the values and attitudes of the Japanese nobility of the early eleventh century.

THE LEGACY OF COLUMBUS
by Sarah Elder Hale, 1992
Page 77

Use with Chapter 14, Lesson 2

Objectives

❑ *Recognize the various points of view concerning the legacy of Columbus.*

❑ *Identify how the voyage of Columbus changed the world.*

❑ *Write a speech for Columbus Day.*

Writing a Speech

After students have read the selection, encourage them to discuss the main idea. *What point does the author make?* (There are differing points of view about what the voyage of Columbus meant to the world—the mingling of the cultures created an exchange that brought about today's cultural diversity; native cultures suffered under Spanish colonialism.) *How did the voyage affect the course of history?* (Europeans came to the Americas in the wake of the voyages and settled the land; the native peoples were displaced as a result of the exploration and settlement.) *Why are cultural exchanges important to history?* (We would not be able to further our understanding of the world around us, and without exchange, cultures would become isolated and stagnant.)

Have students write a speech for Columbus Day. Encourage students to express their point of view in the speech. Have students present their speeches to the class.

BATTLE OF TENOCHTITLÁN
by Aztec Historians, 1521
Pages 78–79

Use with Chapter 14, Lesson 3

Objectives

❑ *Interpret an Aztec pictograph.*

❑ *Create a pictograph of an event.*

Creating Your Own Pictograph

Have students turn to the pictograph on page 79 but have them temporarily cover the explanation that accompanies it. First discuss what a pictograph is and how it uses drawings, many of them symbols, rather than words. Encourage students to speculate about what the figures in this pictograph show. After they have made their own interpretation, have them uncover and read the explanation. Ask students: *Whose version of the battle of Tenochtitlán is this?* (the Aztec version) *How does the pictograph show dates? Locations? Different groups of people?* Use such questions to explore and identify the various symbols that are used.

After the discussion tell each student to choose another event in the history of Latin America and to draw a pictograph that describes it. Encourage them to think in terms of drawn symbols rather than illustrations or written words. Have students exchange pictographs and try to interpret the pictographs drawn by their classmates.

TEARS OF THE INDIANS

by Bartolomé de Las Casas, 1542
Pages 80–81

Use with Chapter 14, Lesson 4

Objectives

- ❏ *Explain the selection's description of the Spanish treatment of the Indians.*
- ❏ *Understand how Las Casas tried to end cruelty toward the Indians.*
- ❏ *Write an interview with Las Casas.*

Rewriting in Another Genre

After students have read Bartolomé de Las Casas's indictment of early Spanish rule in Latin America, explore with the class the accusations that he makes. Ask students: *How does he say the Spanish have mistreated the Indians? What effects has this had on them?* (By making war against and enslaving the Indians, the Spanish had killed large numbers and forced the survivors to live under often intolerable conditions.) Ask students: *How would you say that Las Casas's view of the Indians was different from that of many other Spaniards?* (Las Casas saw them as human souls to be saved; many others treated them as beasts of burden.) *Whom is Las Casas trying to reach with his words?* (fellow Spaniards, especially those with the power to end the cruel treatment of the Indians) *How convincing do you think his arguments are?* (He backs up some of his statements with numbers and he uses very strong language.)

Following this discussion, tell students to act as though they are reporters sent to interview Las Casas about his cause. Have students pair up to write question-and-answer interviews, providing both questions and the possible replies of Las Casas. (For example: *Q:* What can be done to improve the treatment of Indians? *Las Casas:* The Spanish government should impose rules to enforce humane treatment.) Ask pairs of volunteers to take turns reading their interviews to the class, with one person playing the part of the reporter and the other providing Las Casas's answers.

CAPTURED!

by Olaudah Equiano, 1789
Pages 82–83

Use with Chapter 14, Lesson 4

Objectives

- ❏ *Identify the horrors of enslavement as described by Olaudah Equiano.*
- ❏ *Empathize with Equiano's experience.*
- ❏ *Write an editorial criticizing the slave trade.*

Writing an Editorial

After students have read the selection, encourage them to discuss their reactions to it. Have them think about the fright of young children who were kidnapped and taken away from their families to be sold into slavery. Explain to the class that the harmful effects of the slave trade did not end with the separation of young children from their families. Tell students that, like millions of other people who were kidnapped from Africa, young Olaudah Equiano and his sister suffered a long, dangerous ocean voyage in the cramped hold of a ship. Most of those who survived such voyages faced lifetimes of overwork and harsh treatment as well as repeated forced separations from loved ones.

Have students suppose that they are the editors of an antislavery newspaper who are writing an editorial criticizing the slave trade and calling for its end. Explain to students that editorials are newspaper articles that give the opinion of the newspaper's editors about some issue. Students should research the effects of this trade both on people who were sold into slavery and on African society. Have students share their editorials with the class.

THE STOWAWAY
by Karen Hess
Pages 84–87

Objectives

❑ *Trace* Endeavour's *voyage on a map.*

❑ *Recognize the characteristics that make this selection historical fiction.*

❑ *Write a fictionalized diary entry to extend the story.*

Writing a Fictionalized Diary Entry

After students have completed the selection, ask them to identify the location of the different places identified in each diary entry. Using a classroom map or globe, have students trace the voyage of the *Endeavour* from Plymouth, England to the Isle of Madeira. Help students use the map scale to approximate the number of miles the ship traveled. Then, discuss with students the characteristics that make this selection historical fiction. (It is based on real events and is presented in a fictionalized diary format.) Encourage students to identify details that teach them about life in 18th century England. Ask: *Why did the boy stowaway on the* Endeavour? (His father had sent him to work for a butcher because he wouldn't study. The butcher mistreated him.) Point out that this fictionalized diary also presents information about life on board the ship. Ask: *What are some problems the sailors faced?* (They became sick during a severe storm at sea.) *Why did Captain Cook read the Articles of War to the sailors at the beginning of the trip?* (He wanted his crew to know how he expected them to behave during the journey.) *What was the scientific purpose of the voyage?* (They were ordered to observe the planet Venus to determine how far the Earth was from the Sun.)

Divide the class into pairs of students. Have each student pair research additional information about the *Endeavour* voyage. Suggest students use classroom references or the Internet. Encourage them to extend the story by writing another diary entry by the stowaway. Remind students to include factual information as well as the boy's reaction to these real-life events. Call on volunteers to read their diary entries in class.

MARIE ANTOINETTE, PRINCESS OF VERSAILLES
by Kathryn Lasky
Pages 88–90

Objectives

❑ *Evaluate information about a historical figure provided in a fictionalized diary entry.*

❑ *Write an Editorial.*

Writing an Editorial

After students have read the selection, ask them to consider what they learned about Marie Antoinette in this selection. Point out that although the diary entries are fiction, they are based on historical fact. Ask: *What is the purpose of Marie Antoinette's education and training over the next year?* (She is being prepared to marry the French Dauphin and become Queen of France.) *Why does her mother intend to arrange all her children's marriages?* (She wants them to marry royalty and make political alliances.) *How does her sister Caroline feel about her own arranged marriage?* (She feels sad, as indicated in her letter to Marie Antoinette.) *How does Marie Antoinette feel about her own future marriage?* (She seems excited and nervous.) *What do you learn about her character from these diary entries?* (She seems outgoing and inquisitive. Although she is only fourteen, she understands what her role is expected to be.)

Following the discussion, ask students to write an editorial for an Austrian newspaper of the period on the subject of arranged marriages. Bring in examples of editorials from community or school newspapers and encourage students to review them before beginning to write. Point out that a good editorial includes an opinion that is supported by details and facts relating to the subject. Students should review the selection for information that could be used to support their opinions on the topic. Call on volunteers to share their editorials with the class.

LETTER FROM JAMAICA

by Simón Bolívar, 1815
Pages 91–92

Use with Chapter 15, Lesson 2

Objectives

- ❏ *Identify the reasons that Bolívar wanted independence for Spain's American colonies.*
- ❏ *Recognize the role of hyperbole in Bolívar's impassioned plea.*
- ❏ *Write an interview with Simón Bolívar.*

Writing an Interview

After students have read the selection, point out that although Bolívar writes in letter form, his words seem more appropriate to dramatic speech. Write the word *hyperbole* on the chalkboard and tell students that it is a word from literature that refers to exaggeration made for dramatic effect. Encourage students to look through the selection again to find the reasons that Bolívar gives for overthrowing Spain and note his use of hyperbole. (for example, sufferings at the hands of "that unnatural step-mother"; the Spanish military attack on Venezuela made out of "insatiable . . . thirst for blood and crimes"; comparison to "those first monsters who wiped out America's . . . [earliest people]")

As students identify Bolívar's reasons, write them on the chalkboard. Then have students act as journalists from a country outside Latin America. Have pairs of students write interviews with Simon Bolívar in which the questioner tries to find out what Bolívar's specific ideas and criticisms of the Spanish government are. Students should keep in mind that Bolívar was a very daring and passionate man whose answers might be as full of hyperbole as his letters. Have volunteers act out their interviews for the class.

WORKING IN THE MINES

by Ann Eggley and Elizabeth Eggley, 1842
Pages 93–94

Use with Chapter 15, Lesson 3

Objectives

- ❏ *Identify children's working conditions during the Industrial Revolution as described in the selection.*
- ❏ *Identify the Eggleys' description of the effects of such conditions.*
- ❏ *Compare working conditions then and now.*

Linking to Today

As students read this selection, tell them to visualize what is being described and to think what it would be like to work in similar conditions. After they have finished reading, encourage volunteers to share their first impressions. Ask students: *What do you think about Ann's and Elizabeth's lives? What aspects of their lives do you think would be the hardest to endure? Why?* Help students to empathize with the backbreaking, long hours at work, the tiredness, the dirty conditions, and the lack of opportunity for education.

List the conditions that students identify on the chalkboard. Encourage students to compare these conditions with what they know about working conditions today. Opposite each condition on the chalkboard, list students' description of that condition as it is experienced today—for example, 12-hour workday/8-hour workday and only after age 16; no education for children/compulsory school attendance until at least age 16, and so on.

PROGRESS IN INDUSTRY
An Advertisement, 1887
Page 95

Use with Chapter 15, Lesson 3

Objectives

❑ *Identify the effect of the Industrial Revolution on the economy of the United States.*

❑ *Recognize the need for advertising in a growing economy.*

❑ *Write an advertisement for the technology of today.*

Linking to Today

After students have examined the advertisement, ask them to discuss why E. S. Greeley and Company probably came into existence. (With the Industrial Revolution came many inventions, including the steam engine for ships and trains and the telegraph; manufacturers were needed to supply parts for these inventions. The economy grew.) Then encourage students to discuss what they know of advertising. *Why did the E. S. Greeley Company need to advertise?* (Responses will vary somewhat but should include the idea that in a growing economy, suppliers of goods need to show consumers how their products are better than those of their competitors.)

Have students write an advertisement for the technology of today. Advertisements could be for a compact disc, a computer, a video recorder, or another technological product of their choice. You may wish to create a bulletin board of students' advertisements.

CLARA'S DIARY
by Clara Whitney, 1875–1887
Pages 96–97

Use with Chapter 15, Lesson 5

Objectives

❑ *Identify aspects of Japanese culture in the late nineteenth century as seen through the eyes of a young American girl.*

❑ *Write interview questions for Clara about her life in Japan.*

Writing Interview Questions

After students have read the diary entries, discuss some of the observations that Clara made about Japanese culture. *Which events did Clara write about in her diary that showed traditional Japanese culture?* (the Shinto religious ceremony, the celebration of the emperor's birthday, the imperial procession on the day she met the emperor and empress of Japan) *Which events illustrated Japan's modernization?* (the National Exhibition and the opening of the Central Telegraph Office)

Have students work in small groups to come up with interview questions for Clara. Groups should write at least five questions. Then the whole class can decide on the ten best questions and make a plan for finding plausible answers for them. You may wish to have pairs of students take one question and present the interview for their classmates.

ALL QUIET ON THE WESTERN FRONT

by Erich Maria Remarque, 1929
Pages 100–101

Use with Chapter 16, Lesson 1

Objectives

❑ *Explore the realities of trench warfare as described in* All Quiet on the Western Front.

❑ *Recognize the impact of a major piece of antiwar literature from World War I.*

❑ *Write a letter describing trench warfare.*

Rewriting in Another Genre

The American poet Walt Whitman once said, "The real war will never get in the books." However, that was half a century before Erich Maria Remarque wrote *All Quiet on the Western Front.* Tell students that Remarque, who had served in the German Army during World War I, wrote *All Quiet on the Western Front* to describe the horror and futility of war. After students have read this excerpt, help them to understand what a powerful effect Remarque's book had on people of many nations when it came out. Remarque wanted to convince readers that there was nothing noble or glorious about war. Have students discuss how Remarque's book achieved this. (It showed them the horrible side of war.) Ask students: *What adjectives do you think Remarque would use to describe war?* (horrible, frightening, inhuman, and so on) You may wish to point out to the class that Adolf Hitler banned *All Quiet on the Western Front* and hounded Remarque out of Germany because Hitler wanted Germans to embrace war and regard it as glorious.

Tell students to suppose that they are young soldiers in the United States Army during World War I and are experiencing the same kind of trench warfare that Remarque did. Have each student write a letter home, describing a day in the soldier's life. Encourage volunteers to read their letters to the class.

NEVER GIVE UP THE FIGHT

by Winston Churchill and Franklin Roosevelt, 1941
Page 102

Use with Chapter 16, Lesson 3

Objectives

❑ *Recognize how two world leaders used language to comfort and inspire people in the early years of World War II.*

❑ *Present a speech by Roosevelt or Churchill.*

Presenting a Speech

After students have read the quotations and listened to them on the cassette, point out to them that during Word War II both Franklin Roosevelt and Winston Churchill made frequent speeches to the American and British public. *Why did Roosevelt and Churchill make speeches during the war?* (The times were tense, and people of both countries were alarmed; these leaders sought to reassure the public by keeping them informed; they also wanted to bring the people together to face a common enemy.) *What do the words of both leaders have in common?* (They acknowledge the seriousness of the situation and encourage the people to be strong and to have courage.)

Have students find copies of speeches delivered by Churchill and Roosevelt during the war years. Have students practice reading the speeches and then present them to the class. You may wish to tape-record the speeches so that students can listen to them during your study of World War II.

THE ART OF KEEPING COOL
by Janet Taylor Lisle
Pages 103–107

Use with Chapter 16, Lesson 3

Objectives

❏ *Understand the relationships between story characters.*

❏ *Perform the story as Reader's Theater.*

Using Reader's Theater

After students have read the selection, encourage them to talk about the relationships between the story characters. Ask: *Why is Robert afraid that Abel will recognize him in the crowd of boys who throw bottles at him?* (He was the one who talked to the FBI about Abel.) *How would you contrast his grandparents' views of Abel?* (His grandfather thinks that he's dangerous; his grandmother defends him.) *Why doesn't Elliot stand up for Abel when his grandfather threatens him?* (He seems afraid of his grandfather.) *How would you describe the relationship between Robert and Elliot?* (They seem close, even though they have different opinions of Abel.)

Divide the class into small groups. Ask each group to select a scene from the story excerpt to present as Reader's Theater. Students should take the roles of different story characters, while one of them reads the narration. Have each group select a student director. After students have rehearsed their dramatization, invite them to perform their scenes in class.

THE WAR YEARS IN VIETNAM
by Le Ly Hayslip, 1989
Pages 108–110

Use with Chapter 16, Lesson 5

Objectives

❏ *Appreciate how Le Ly Hayslip's family was a source of strength for her during wartime.*

❏ *Understand how a Vietnamese woman is fulfilling goals set in childhood.*

Writing About Goals

After students have read the selection, help them to see how Le Ly Hayslip's childhood in Vietnam affected her as an adult. Remind students that Le Ly Hayslip's role models were her father and her heroic ancestor, Phung Thi Chinh. Have students discuss what she learned from them. (resourcefulness, love of country, concern for others, the will to overcome obstacles) Ask students: *What goals did Le Ly Hayslip and her father develop for her?* (to stay alive, to protect others, and to live in peace) *What is Le Ly Hayslip doing today?* (living in California, where she founded a charitable relief and world peace group)

Ask students to think about the people whom they admire and the personal qualities that make these people admirable. Suggest that these might be relatives, public figures, or people from the past. Have students write a paragraph explaining what they might learn from the example set by these people. The paragraphs should state some personal goals and explain how the students might fulfill them. Have volunteers share their paragraphs with the class.

GANDHI
by Leonard Everett Fisher
Pages 111–115

Use with Chapter 17, Lesson 1

Objectives
- ❑ *Recognize the elements of a biography.*
- ❑ *Identify the events that influenced Gandhi's beliefs.*
- ❑ *Link Gandhi's ideas to more recent political movements.*

Linking to Today

After students have read the selection, point out to them that it is an excerpt from a biography. A **biography** is the story of a person's life told by another person. Ask students to explain the difference between a biography and an autobiography. (An autobiography is the story of a person's life told by that person.) Ask: *What is one important difference between having another person describe important events in someone's life and having the same events told by the individual?* (Another person wouldn't know how the person thought and felt about the events.) Then ask students: *What important event influenced Gandhi when he was a child?* (His father was imprisoned by the British for defending an Indian prince whom they had insulted.) *What event influenced Gandhi after he moved to South Africa?* (In South Africa he was thrown off a train for refusing to sit in the baggage car.)

Explain that Gandhi believed in civil disobedience, the peaceful refusal to obey a law or laws as a protest against injustice. Explain to the class that Gandhi's beliefs have influenced people in many parts of the world, including the United States. Divide the class into small groups. Ask each group to find an example of a speech made by Gandhi and by the civil rights leader, Martin Luther King, Jr., in which they discuss their beliefs about equality and justice. Invite students to read the speeches and compare the ideas expressed in each one. Then, call on the students in each group to read parts of the speeches aloud to the class. If time permits, play a recording of the "I Have A Dream" oration by Dr. Martin Luther King, Jr., Explain that Dr. King gave this speech on August 28, 1963, when he addressed more than 250,000 civil rights marchers from the steps of the Lincoln Memorial in Washington, D.C.

ROAD TO PEACE
by Yasir Arafat and Yitzhak Rabin, 1993 and 1995
Pages 116–118

Use with Chapter 17, Lesson 2

Objectives
- ❑ *Recognize how two world leaders addressed their hopes for peace in the Middle East.*
- ❑ *Understand past conflicts between Israel and Palestine.*
- ❑ *Write an editorial presenting a point of view about the issue of peace in the Middle East.*

Writing an Editorial

After students have read and heard the speeches, discuss the points of view expressed by each leader. (Both leaders are happy that the two countries have reached an agreement; Rabin seems especially mindful of past hostilities in his speeches; both leaders know that the road to peace will take exceptional courage and perseverance.) Point out that these speeches were made in September 1993 and September 1995. Ask students what significant event has occurred since then. (Rabin was assassinated by one of his countrymen who opposed the peace agreement with Palestine.)

Have students conduct further research into the Palestinian/Israeli conflicts over land in the Middle East. Based on their findings, encourage students to write an editorial about one of the issues that emerged. For example, students could support Israeli claims, Palestinian claims, or a compromise position. Suggest that students share their editorials with the class.

U. S ATTACKED

NY Times **Headline from September 12, 2001**
Page 119

Use with Chapter 17, Lesson 2

Objectives

❑ *Understand the impact of the events that took place on September 11, 2001.*

❑ *Write a poem that expresses personal feelings about the attack and its aftermath.*

Writing a Poem

After students have read the headlines, discuss the impact of the terrorist attacks on Americans. Ask: *What do you think people thought when they saw this headline?* Point out that Americans responded to the attack in a variety of ways, including donating money to charities that helped the victims, writing letters, and making drawings to express their feelings about the event. Ask: *What were the different ways in which Americans were affected by the events of September 11? In what way do you think the attacks brought Americans together?* (Answers will vary.)

Divide the class into pairs of students. Invite each student pair to research the events of September 11 in classroom encyclopedias or on the Internet. Have students use this selection and their research to compose a poem expressing their personal thoughts about the terrorist attacks and their aftermath. Encourage students to share their poems with the class.

THE VISION THAT I SEE

by Kwame Nkrumah, 1953
Pages 120–121

Use with Chapter 17, Lesson 3

Objectives

❑ *Identify Kwame Nkrumah's goals for Africans as conveyed in his speech.*

❑ *Create a personal vision for Africa.*

Writing Your Own Speech

After students have read the speech, help them to identify its main idea. Ask students: *If you had to state the major theme of Nkrumah's vision, what would it be?* (Answers will vary but should touch on the idea of self-determination.) *How does Nkrumah use examples from history to enrich his vision?* (He gives examples of African achievements to show that great things are possible; he also gives examples of people enduring great suffering.) *What does Nkrumah think will help bring about his vision?* (fighting to end colonialism and imperialism in order to bring about equality) List students' responses on the chalkboard and discuss each of the ideas with the class. Ask students if these ideas remind them of the personal visions of any people from other countries.

Have students suppose that they are Africans who want a better life for people in their countries. Ask students what their goals for the future might be. Have students write a short speech expressing their goals. Students may wish to look up an African country of their choosing in the encyclopedia to find detailed historical examples for their speeches. Encourage volunteers to share their speeches with the class.

LONG WALK TO FREEDOM
by **Nelson Mandela, 1994**
Pages 122–124

Use with Chapter 18, Lesson 2

Objectives

- ❏ *Recognize the elements of an autobiography.*
- ❏ *Identify the hardships that Nelson Mandela faced on his "road to freedom."*
- ❏ *Compare the treatment of political prisoners in South Africa to the treatment of those in other countries.*

Writing Paragraphs of Comparison

After students have read the selection, point out to them that this selection is an autobiography. An **autobiography** is the story of a person's life told by the person. Ask students to tell how an autobiography is different from a biography. (A biography is the story of a person's life told by another person.) Then ask students to discuss some of the hardships Mandela faced while he was a political prisoner in South Africa. (He had to work long hours in the lime quarry without sunglasses to protect his eyes from the glare; he was not allowed to read newspapers; he faced solitary confinement and no food for breaking the rules.) *What was Mandela's goal when he got out of prison?* (to liberate both the oppressed and the oppressor)

Have students think about some of the other selections in the Anthology that deal with political imprisonment (*The Endless Steppe, No Tears for Mao*, for example) and write a paragraph comparing the treatment of political prisoners. Encourage students to share their paragraphs with the class.

AMPHIBIANS IN DANGER
by **Ron Fridell**
Pages 125–127

Use with Geography

Objectives

- ❏ *Understand the factors responsible for the decline in the amphibian population.*
- ❏ *Create an ad campaign to promote awareness of environmental dangers to amphibians.*

Creating an Ad Campaign to Promote Environmental Awareness

After students have read the selection, discuss the factors responsible for the extinction of many amphibian species. Ask: *Why does the greenhouse effect endanger amphibians?* (The greenhouse effect heats up the atmosphere. Amphibians, which are cold-blooded, need relatively stable conditions to survive. If ponds and streams dry up, their eggs and tadpoles will die.) *What are some other global climate changes that scientists predict?* (more extreme weather; more floods and droughts; more Arctic ice melting) *What other environmental dangers face amphibians?* (acid rain, snow, and chemical pesticides) Discuss the importance of continuing to study our natural world. Point out that scientists' efforts to understand why amphibians are dying out all over the world is one example of this. Ask: *Why do you think it's important for scientists to continue to collect data about these environmental problems?* (to better understand their affect on amphibians and other living things) *Why do you think that amphibians were described in this book as acting "as environmental monitors"?* (They are more susceptible to changes in the natural world because they are in closer contact with the environment than other animals. The problems affecting the amphibians will eventually affect human beings.)

Divide the class into small groups. Ask each group to create an ad campaign to make students and members of the community aware of these environmental dangers to amphibians. Each group can decide on the form their campaign will take, such as posters, slogans, leaflets, and booklets. Have students do additional research in classroom encyclopedias and on the Internet. Call on different groups to present their campaigns in c Display the posters in the classroom.